Cold War
Reference Library
Cumulative Index

Cold War
Reference Library
Cumulative Index

Cumulates Indexes For:

Cold War: Almanac
Cold War: Biographies
Cold War: Primary Sources

Lawrence W. Baker,
Project Editor

Detroit • New York • San Diego • San Francisco • Cleveland • New Haven, Conn. • Waterville, Maine • London • Munich

Cold War Reference Library Cumulative Index

Project Editor
Lawrence W. Baker

Editorial
Diane Sawinski

Permissions
Margaret Chamberlain, Shalice Shah-Caldwell

Imaging and Multimedia
Leitha Etheridge-Sims, Mary Grimes, Lezlie Light, Mike Logusz, Dave Oblender, Kelly A. Quin

Product Design
Pamela A. E. Galbreath, Jennifer Wahi

Composition
Evi Seoud

Manufacturing
Rita Wimberley

LIBRARY OF CONGRESS CATALOGING-IN-PUBLICATION DATA

Cold War reference library cumulative index / Lawrence W. Baker, index coordinator.

p. cm. — (UXL Cold War reference library)

Summary: A cumulative index for materials in a series on the Cold War era.

ISBN 0-7876-7667-5

1. Hanes, Sharon M. Cold War—Juvenile literature—Indexes. 2. Cold War—Biography—Juvenile literature—Indexes. 3. Cold War—History—Sources—Juvenile literature—Indexes. 4. World politics—1945–1989—Sources—Juvenile literature—Indexes. 5. United States—Foreign relations—Soviet Union—Juvenile literature—Indexes. 6. Soviet Union—Foreign relations—United States—Juvenile literature—Indexes. [1. Cold War—History—Sources. 2. United States—Foreign relations—Soviet Union—Indexes. 3. Soviet Union—Foreign relations—United States—Indexes.] I. Baker, Lawrence W. II. Series.

D843 .C577322 2003
016.90982'5—dc22

2003019278

Printed in the United States of America
10 9 8 7 6 5 4 3 2 1

Cold War Reference Library Cumulative Index

CWA1 = Cold War: Almanac, volume 1
CWA2 = Cold War: Almanac, volume 2
CWB1 = Cold War: Biographies, volume 1
CWB2 = Cold War: Biographies, volume 2
CWPS = Cold War: Primary Sources

A

Gromyko, Andrey, and
CWB1: 164
Reagan, Ronald, and
CWA2: 340, 355;
CWB2: 392–93
Sakharov, Andrey, and
CWB2: 413
Shevardnadze, Eduard,
and *CWB2:* 420
Soviet Union and *CWA2:*
335–36, 337, 351,
355–56; *CWB1:* 50, 70,
78, 156, 164; *CWB2:*
252, 392–93, 413, 420
Africa *CWA2:* 206–8,
325–27; *CWB2:* 310,
470. *See also* Middle
East specific countries
African Americans *CWA2:*
279 (ill.)
Black Power and *CWA2:*
276, 281–82
Carter, Jimmy, and
CWB1: 71, 73
discrimination and
CWB2: 402–3
economy and *CWA2:* 278,
281, 282
freedom and *CWA2:*
275–76
Hoover, J. Edgar, and
CWB1: 192
military draft and *CWA2:*
285
poverty and *CWB1:* 201–3
racism and *CWA2:*
275–76, 278–83, 285
Red Scare and *CWA1:* 115
segregation and *CWA2:*
278–79, 281; *CWB1:*
68, 71, 73; *CWB2:*
·221–22
separatism and *CWA2:* 281
Truman, Harry S., and
CWB2: 460
violence and *CWA2:*
281–82
Agent Orange *CWA2:* 283
Agnew, Spiro *CWA2:* 310
Agriculture. *See also* Economy
in Chile *CWB1:* 21–22
in China *CWB1:* 121–22
in Cuba *CWB1:* 86

economy and *CWPS:* 46
Khrushchev, Nikita, and
CWPS: 189, 193, 199
in Soviet Union *CWB1:*
44, 46; *CWB2:* 232,
238, 239, 278, 348, 429;
CWPS: 175, 181, 189,
199
Stalin, Joseph, and
CWB2: 429; *CWPS:*
181
in United States of America *CWPS:* 199
Akhromeyev, Marshall
CWPS: 312
Albert Einstein Peace Prize
CWB2: 216, 343
Albright, Madeleine *CWB2:*
403
Alexander I *CWA1:* 186
Alien Enemy Bureau *CWB1:*
187
Alien Registration Act. *See*
Smith Act
Allende, Salvador *CWA2:*
308; *CWB1:* 17 (ill.),
17–24, 21 (ill.); *CWB2:*
263–64, 362
Alliance for Progress *CWA1:*
177; *CWA2:* 252,
262–63
Allied Control Council
CWA1: 56, 60–61
Allies
definition of *CWA1:* 2
peace treaty and *CWA2:*
364
World War II and *CWA1:*
8–18, 48, 55, 105
Alliluyeva, Svetlana *CWB2:*
433, 435
All-Russian Communist
Party. *See* Communist
Party
"American Relations with
the Soviet Union." *See*
Clifford-Elsey Report
American Society of Newspaper Editors *CWPS:*
89, 99
American Youth for Democracy. *See* Young Communist League

Ames, Aldrich *CWA1:* 157,
162
Anastasio Somoza, Luis
CWA1: 180
Andropov, Yuri *CWA2:* 344,
348, 349; *CWPS:* 283
Brezhnev, Leonid, and
CWB1: 45
Communist Party and
CWB2: 417
death of *CWB1:* 45, 152;
CWB2: 395, 417
economy and *CWB2:* 417
election of *CWB1:* 45,
152
Gorbachev, Mikhail, and
CWB1: 152–53; *CWB2:*
417
Harriman, W. Averell, and
CWB1: 175
Komsomol and *CWB1:* 45
Reagan, Ronald, and
CWB1: 155
Sakharov, Andrey, and
CWB2: 413
Shevardnadze, Eduard,
and *CWB2:* 417
Andrus, Cecil *CWA2:* 322
(ill.)
Angleton, James Jesús
CWA1: 154
Angola *CWA2:* 308, 326–27;
CWB1: 50, 164
Antiballistic missiles (ABM)
CWA2: 247, 258, 303;
CWB2: 361; *CWPS:*
287–88
Anti-Radical Division
CWA1: 102–3. *See also*
Federal Bureau of Investigation (FBI)
ANZUS Pact *CWA1:* 50;
CWB1: 128
Apartheid *CWB2:* 310
Arabs *CWA2:* 328–30;
CWB1: 36–37. *See also*
specific countries
Arbenz Guzmán, Jacobo
CWA1: 169, 179–80
Argentina *CWA2:* 324;
CWB1: 76
Armistice of Panmunjan
CWA1: 50 (ill.)

Arms race. *See* Nuclear weapons, race for

Armstrong, Neil A. *CWA2:* 199, 199 (ill.)

Army-McCarthy hearings *CWB2:* 335

Arzamas-16 *CWA1:* 89–90; *CWB2:* 286, 287, 409

Ashurst, Henry F. *CWB1:* 190 (ill.)

Asia
  communism and *CWPS:* 211
  containment and *CWPS:* 62, 65–66, 67–68, 81, 264
  economy of *CWPS:* 271, 272
  MacArthur, Douglas, and *CWPS:* 81, 82–84
  nationalism in *CWPS:* 271
  Nixon Doctrine and *CWPS:* 264, 268–73, 276
  Nixon, Richard M., and *CWPS:* 264, 267–73, 276
  peace and *CWPS:* 107, 270–71, 277
  Soviet Union and *CWPS:* 68
  war and *CWPS:* 270, 277

Aswan High Dam *CWA2:* 203

Asymmetrical response *CWA1:* 173–75

"At Historic Crossroads: Documents on the December 1989 Malta Summit" *CWPS:* 307–18

Atlas Shrugged CWB2: 383–84

Atomic bombs *CWPS:* 69, 115, 116. *See also* Nuclear weapons
  definition of *CWA1:* 80, 88
  development of *CWA1:* 9, 80–84, 87, 88–91; *CWA2:* 244; *CWB1:* 31, 38; *CWB2:* 212, 283, 285–88, 351, 366, 371–72, 432, 433, 458

hydrogen bombs and *CWA1:* 92–95
  testing of *CWA1:* 13–14, 43, 79–80, 85–86, 90, 91, 115; *CWB1:* 6, 31, 106, 108; *CWB2:* 285, 287–88, 333, 366, 371, 372, 373, 434, 458
  use of *CWA1:* 17, 86–88, 135; *CWA2:* 219, 241; *CWB1:* 3, 31; *CWB2:* 285, 297, 371, 372, 409, 432, 458

Atomic Energy Commission (AEC) *CWA1:* 80, 92, 93–94; *CWA2:* 242–43; *CWB1:* 3; *CWB2:* 373–75

"Atoms for Peace" *CWA2:* 241; *CWB1:* 140–41. *See also* "Peaceful Uses of Atomic Energy" speech

Attlee, Clement R. *CWA1:* 3, 15, 16 (ill.), 86; *CWB1:* 25 (ill.), **25–32,** 30 (ill.); *CWPS:* 16
  Bevin, Ernest, and *CWB1:* 31, 33, 35
  election of *CWB1:* 27, 33, 36, 106
  Potsdam Conference and *CWB1:* 28, 35–36, 66; *CWB2:* 431

Australia *CWA1:* 50

Austria *CWA1:* 185

Azerbaijan (Iran) *CWA1:* 20

B

B-28 bombs *CWA2:* 242–43, 243 (ill.)

B-47 aircraft *CWA2:* 237 (ill.)

B-52 aircraft *CWA2:* 238, 242–43

Baby boom *CWA2:* 286–87

Back channel negotiations *CWA2:* 300, 301

Baghdad Pact *CWA2:* 202, 204; *CWB1:* 130, 132. *See also* Central Treaty Organization (CENTO)

Baker, James A. *CWB1:* 57; *CWB2:* 420–21, 421 (ill.); *CWPS:* 305, 307

Balaguer, Joaquín *CWA2:* 265

Ball, George *CWB1:* 7 (ill.)

Ballistic Missile Early Warning Systems (BMEWS) *CWA2:* 239 (ill.), 240

Ballistic missiles *CWPS:* 287–88, 302–3

Baltic States *CWA1:* 7; *CWA2:* 361–62, 367, 369; *CWB1:* 57; *CWPS:* 317–18, 320

Ban the Bomb marches *CWA2:* 245–46

Baruch, Bernard *CWA1:* 3, 22; *CWB1:* 3, 64, 126; *CWB2:* 373

Baruch Plan *CWB1:* 3

Basic Principle of Relations between the United States and Soviet Union *CWA2:* 304

Batista y Zaldívar, Fulgencio *CWA1:* 180; *CWA2:* 208, 215, 258; *CWB1:* 84–85

Battle of Normandy *CWB1:* 136

Battle of Stalingrad *CWB2:* 233

Battle of the Bulge *CWB1:* 136

Bay of Pigs *CWA2:* 214, 217–18, 218 (ill.), 252, 258–59; *CWB1:* 87, 113, 144; *CWB2:* 223, 340–41; *CWPS:* 233

BBC *CWA1:* 143

BCCI scandal *CWB1:* 114–15

Begin, Menachem *CWA2:* 329 (ill.), 329; *CWB1:* 78 (ill.), 79

Belarus *CWA2:* 370, 373

Belgium *CWA1:* 37; *CWA2:* 207–8

Benes, Edvard *CWA1:* 34–35, 35 (ill.)

Blunt, Anthony F. *CWA1:* 128, 142, 143, 144; *CWPS:* 50

BMEWS. *See* Ballistic Missile Early Warning Systems (BMEWS)

Boeing Aircraft *CWA2:* 238

Bogart, Humphrey *CWPS:* 143 (ill.)

BOI. *See* Bureau of Investigation (BOI)

Boland Amendments *CWA2:* 332

Bolshevik Revolution *CWPS:* 2. *See also* Bolsheviks

communism and *CWA1:* 2, 3–5, 6–7; *CWB1:* 187; *CWB2:* 231, 380–81

Communist Party and *CWB1:* 45

economy and *CWA1:* 6

February Revolution *CWB2:* 347

freedom and *CWA1:* 100–101

Gromyko, Andrey, and *CWB1:* 159–60

KGB (Soviet secret police) and *CWA1:* 132

Khrushchev, Nikita, and *CWB2:* 231

Kosygin, Aleksey, and *CWB2:* 277–78

Lenin, Vladimir I., and *CWA1:* 6–7; *CWB2:* 278, 347, 427

Molotov, Vyacheslav, and *CWB2:* 346–47

October Revolution *CWB2:* 347

Rand, Ayn, and *CWB2:* 380–81

Red Scare and *CWA1:* 101–3

Stalin, Joseph, and *CWB2:* 346, 347, 427–28

success of *CWB1:* 42

Tito, Josip Broz, and *CWB2:* 445

Wilson, Woodrow, and *CWA1:* 4–5

Bolsheviks *CWA1:* 2, 3–5, 6–7, 120. *See also* Bolshevik Revolution

Bonn (West Germany) *CWA1:* 67

Bonner, Yelena *CWB2:* 408, 412 (ill.), 412–13, 413–14, 415

Books *CWA1:* 118

Borden, William L. *CWB2:* 376

Boyce, Christopher *CWA1:* 154–55, 155 (ill.)

Bradley, Omar *CWPS:* 86

Brady, James *CWB2:* 392

Brandeis, Louis D. *CWB1:* 2

Branden, Barbara *CWB2:* 384

Branden, Nathaniel *CWB2:* 384

Brandt, Willy *CWA2:* 299, 305–6, 306 (ill.); *CWB1:* 15, 15 (ill.), 48

Brazil *CWA2:* 263–64, 324; *CWB1:* 76

Bretton Woods Conference *CWA1:* 13; *CWB1:* 2–3

Brezhnev Doctrine *CWA2:* 298, 300, 358; *CWB1:* 47; *CWPS:* 274

Brezhnev, Leonid *CWA1:* 172 (ill.); *CWA2:* 305 (ill.), 331 (ill.); *CWB1:* 41 (ill.), **41–52**, 48 (ill.), 49 (ill.); *CWB2:* 240 (ill.), 362 (ill.); *CWPS:* 264–65, 274, 280

ABM treaty and *CWB2:* 262

Afghanistan and *CWB1:* 50

Africa and *CWA2:* 325–27

Andropov, Yuri, and *CWB1:* 45

Angola and *CWB1:* 50

Brandt, Willy, and *CWB1:* 48

Brezhnev Doctrine and *CWA2:* 300; *CWB1:* 47

Carter, Jimmy, and *CWA2:* 316, 330; *CWB1:* 49, 50, 74–75

character of *CWB1:* 41, 46, 47

Chernenko, Konstantin, and *CWB1:* 44, 45

China and *CWB1:* 47

Communist Party and *CWB1:* 41, 42, 43–46, 49–50

coup d'état and *CWB1:* 45–46

Czechoslovakia and *CWA2:* 268; *CWB1:* 43, 47; *CWB2:* 282

death of *CWA2:* 348; *CWB1:* 45, 51, 152; *CWB2:* 395, 417

détente and *CWA2:* 310, 311; *CWB1:* 48–49; *CWB2:* 360–61

Dubcek, Alexander, and *CWA2:* 268; *CWB1:* 47

early life of *CWB1:* 42–43, 45

economy and *CWB1:* 46, 51

Egypt and *CWB1:* 50

election of *CWA2:* 255–56; *CWB1:* 41, 45

Ethiopia and *CWB1:* 50

on Europe *CWB1:* 41

as first secretary *CWB2:* 240

Ford, Gerald, and *CWA2:* 314; *CWB1:* 48–49

freedom and *CWB1:* 46, 47

Gorbachev, Mikhail, and *CWB1:* 152

Great Terror and *CWB1:* 42–43

Gromyko, Andrey, and *CWB1:* 164, 166

health of *CWA2:* 349

Helsinki Accords and *CWA2:* 314; *CWB2:* 413

human rights and *CWA2:* 323–24; *CWB1:* 75

Israel and *CWB1:* 50

Jews and *CWB1:* 75

KGB (Soviet secret police) and *CWB1:* 46

Khrushchev, Nikita, and *CWB1:* 43, 44–46; *CWB2:* 238
Kissinger, Henry, and *CWB2:* 261–62
Komsomol and *CWB1:* 42
Kosygin, Aleksey, and *CWB2:* 280, 282
military and *CWB1:* 47, 51
Moldavia and *CWB1:* 43–44
nation building and *CWA2:* 325–27; *CWB1:* 50
Nixon, Richard M., and *CWA2:* 273, 304, 307; *CWB1:* 48–49, 50; *CWB2:* 261–62, 360–61
nuclear weapons and *CWA2:* 256–58, 304, 305, 323, 330, 336–37; *CWB1:* 47, 48–49, 77–78, 166; *CWB2:* 360–61
October War and *CWB1:* 50
Palestine Liberation Organization and *CWB1:* 50
Poland and *CWB1:* 51
Reagan, Ronald, and *CWB1:* 51
Romania and *CWB1:* 43
Somalia and *CWB1:* 50
space programs and *CWB1:* 47
Stalin, Joseph, and *CWB1:* 44
Strategic Arms Limitation Talks (SALT) and *CWA2:* 304, 323, 330; *CWB1:* 49, 50, 77–78, 166; *CWB2:* 261, 360–61
Syria and *CWB1:* 50
Third World and *CWB1:* 50
Vietnam War and *CWB1:* 50
Warsaw Pact and *CWB1:* 47–48
West Germany and *CWB1:* 47–48

World War II and *CWB1:* 43
Brinkmanship *CWB1:* 128–29, 130; *CWPS:* 119–20, 190–91
asymmetrical response and *CWA1:* 173–75
definition of *CWA1:* 167, 168
Eisenhower Doctrine and *CWA2:* 203–5
Eisenhower, Dwight D., and *CWA2:* 203–4
Kennedy, John F., and *CWA2:* 256
New Look and *CWA1:* 173–75
nuclear weapons and *CWA1:* 167, 168, 169, 184
British Broadcasting Corporation (BBC) *CWA1:* 143
British Commonwealth of Nations *CWB1:* 29
British Empire *CWB1:* 25, 29
Browder, Earl *CWPS:* 160
Brown, Harold *CWA2:* 321, 322 (ill.)
Brown, Pat *CWB2:* 390
Brown v. Board of Education of Topeka CWA2: 278–79; *CWB1:* 68
Brugioni, Dino A. *CWPS:* 250, 259
Brussels Pact *CWA1:* 37; *CWB1:* 38
Brzezinski, Zbigniew *CWA2:* 321, 327–28, 335; *CWB1:* 74, 75, 75 (ill.)
Budget *CWPS:* 102, 119–20, 324
Bulganin, Nikolay *CWA1:* 177; *CWA2:* 197; *CWB2:* 233, 234, 290 (ill.)
Bulgaria *CWA1:* 18
Bullitt, William C. *CWB2:* 209
Bundy, McGeorge *CWA2:* 221; *CWPS:* 236

Bureau of Investigation (BOI). *See* Federal Bureau of Investigation
Burgess, Guy *CWA1:* 128, 142, 143; *CWPS:* 50
Bush, Barbara *CWB1:* 54, 61
Bush, George *CWA2:* 363 (ill.); *CWB1:* 53 (ill.), **53–61,** 59 (ill.); *CWPS:* 305 (ill.), 308 (ill.), 310 (ill.), 322 (ill.)
"At Historic Crossroads: Documents on the December 1989 Malta Summit" *CWPS:* 307–18
as author *CWB1:* 61
Baker, James, and *CWB2:* 421; *CWPS:* 307
Baltic States and *CWA2:* 369
Carter, Jimmy, and *CWB1:* 55, 81
Central Intelligence Agency and *CWB1:* 55
chemical weapons and *CWPS:* 311
Cheney, Richard, and *CWPS:* 305
China and *CWA2:* 362; *CWB1:* 55
Cold War and *CWA2:* 347
Cold War's end and *CWPS:* 296–97, 319–25
democracy and *CWA2:* 369
disarmament and *CWPS:* 303–4, 305, 308, 311, 322, 323
early life of *CWB1:* 53–54
economy and *CWA2:* 362; *CWPS:* 308, 309–11, 323, 324–25
election of *CWA2:* 356; *CWB1:* 56; *CWB2:* 399, 420; *CWPS:* 294–95, 324–25
"End of Cold War: Address Before a Joint Session of the Congress on the State of the Union, January 28, 1992" *CWPS:* 319–26

Ford, Gerald, and *CWB1:* 55

freedom and *CWPS:* 315, 320, 323

Germany and *CWA2:* 363–64; *CWB2:* 405; *CWPS:* 317

Goldwater, Barry, and *CWB1:* 54

Gorbachev, Mikhail, and *CWA2:* 347, 356–57, 362–64, 368, 369, 372; *CWB1:* 57, 58, 157; *CWB2:* 405; *CWPS:* 283, 294–97, 300, 303–4, 305, 307–18

honors for *CWB1:* 54

imperialism and *CWB1:* 59

Iran-Contra scandal and *CWA2:* 332–33; *CWB1:* 56, 60; *CWB2:* 398

Iraq and *CWA2:* 365; *CWB1:* 60

isolationism and *CWPS:* 323

Kennan, George F., and *CWB2:* 217

Kissinger, Henry, and *CWA2:* 356; *CWB2:* 266

Kohl, Helmut, and *CWB2:* 274

military and *CWB1:* 54, 58; *CWPS:* 320, 322–23

Nixon, Richard M., and *CWB1:* 55; *CWB2:* 364

Noriega, Manuel, and *CWB1:* 59

North Atlantic Treaty Organization (NATO) and *CWA2:* 363–64

nuclear weapons and *CWA2:* 356–57, 362, 368, 369–70, 372; *CWB1:* 57, 58; *CWPS:* 295, 296, 303–4, 311, 320, 322–23

oil and *CWB1:* 54

Organization of American States and *CWB1:* 60

Panama and *CWB1:* 59–60

perestroika and *CWPS:* 309

Persian Gulf War and *CWB1:* 60; *CWPS:* 317, 324

power and *CWPS:* 320, 321–22

presidency of *CWB1:* 56–60

Reagan, Ronald, and *CWA2:* 256; *CWB2:* 391; *CWPS:* 283, 294–95

Republican Party and *CWB1:* 54, 55

retirement of *CWB1:* 61

Rice, Condoleezza, and *CWB2:* 401, 404–5

Russia and *CWB1:* 58–59

Somalia and *CWB1:* 60

Soviet collapse and *CWA2:* 369–70

Soviet Union and *CWA2:* 369–70; *CWB1:* 57, 58; *CWB2:* 420, 421; *CWPS:* 294–97, 303–4, 305, 307–18

Strategic Air Command (SAC) and *CWA2:* 369; *CWPS:* 320, 323

Strategic Arms Reduction Talks (START) and *CWA2:* 357

Texas and *CWB1:* 54–55

Ukraine and *CWB1:* 58

United Nations and *CWB1:* 55, 60

on United States of America *CWB1:* 53

vice presidency of *CWB1:* 55–56; *CWPS:* 283, 295

Watergate scandal and *CWB1:* 55

World War II and *CWB1:* 54

Yeltsin, Boris, and *CWA2:* 369; *CWB1:* 58–59; *CWPS:* 322, 323

Bush, George W. *CWB1:* 61; *CWB2:* 253, 401, 406 (ill.), 406–7; *CWPS:* 285

Bush, Jeb *CWB1:* 61

Bush, Vannevar *CWA1:* 83

Byrnes, James F. *CWA1:* 3, 16, 18, 20, 31; *CWB1:* 3, 62 (ill.), **62–69,** 67 (ill.), 127; *CWPS:* 12, 13, 28, 29

C

Cambodia *CWA1:* 181–82; *CWA2:* 327, 328

Cambridge Spies *CWA1:* 135, 140–44; *CWPS:* 50

Cameras *CWA1:* 136, 137 (ill.)

Camp David *CWA2:* 201

Camp David Accords *CWA2:* 328–30, 329 (ill.); *CWB1:* 70, 78 (ill.), 78–79; *CWB2:* 263

Campaign for Nuclear Disarmament (CND) *CWA2:* 245–46

Candy *CWA1:* 66

Capitalism

Cold War and *CWA1:* 25, 60; *CWB2:* 384–85

colonialism and *CWB1:* 178–79

Cominform and *CWPS:* 45

communism and *CWA1:* 19, 23–24, 25, 29, 33, 129, 169–70, 188; *CWA2:* 215–16, 352; *CWB1:* 111, 150, 181, 186; *CWB2:* 210–11, 237, 251, 272, 351, 357, 385, 433–34; *CWPS:* 5, 11, 48, 99, 128, 148, 149, 301–2, 305

definition of *CWA1:* 28, 56, 126, 168; *CWA2:* 192, 214, 298, 320, 348

democracy and *CWA2:* 299, 320; *CWB1:* 42

dictatorship and *CWB1:* 84–85, 99

economy and *CWA1:* 4, 27, 28, 56, 58, 104, 126, 168, 169–70; *CWA2:* 192, 214, 216, 298, 299, 320, 348, 372–73;

CWB1: 3, 26, 42, 86, 111, 119, 127, 150, 178; *CWB2:* 211, 237, 251–52, 313, 385, 404; *CWPS:* 1

Europe and *CWPS:* 2–3

facism and *CWB1:* 186

Germany and *CWA1:* 58–59

Gorbachev, Mikhail, and *CWA2:* 352

Great Depression and *CWA1:* 104

Ho Chi Minh and *CWB1:* 178–79

imperialism and *CWA2:* 208, 215; *CWPS:* 27, 74

Indochina and *CWB1:* 181

Kennan, George F., and *CWB2:* 211

Khrushchev, Nikita, and *CWA1:* 188; *CWPS:* 196

Kosygin, Aleksey, and *CWB2:* 280–82

Mao Zedong and *CWB2:* 313

Marshall Plan and *CWA1:* 31–32

nation building and *CWA1:* 177, 178–79

objectivism and *CWB2:* 382

property and *CWA1:* 4, 27, 28, 56, 58, 101, 126, 128, 168, 169; *CWA2:* 192, 214, 216, 298, 299, 320, 348; *CWB1:* 3, 42, 86, 111, 150, 178; *CWB2:* 211, 237, 251–52, 313, 385, 404; *CWPS:* 1

Rand, Ayn, and *CWB2:* 385

Russia and *CWA2:* 373

Soviet Union and *CWA2:* 304, 352, 361, 367–68; *CWB2:* 280–82

Stalin, Joseph, and *CWB2:* 210–11, 351

United States of America and *CWB1:* 86, 127

West Germany and *CWB2:* 268

Yeltsin, Boris, and *CWA2:* 367–68

Carmichael, Stokely *CWA2:* 276, 281

Cars *CWA1:* 137

Carter Center *CWB1:* 80

Carter Doctrine *CWA2:* 336

Carter, Jimmy *CWA2:* 322 (ill.), 329 (ill.), 331 (ill.); *CWB1:* 70 (ill.), **70–81,** 78 (ill.); *CWB2:* 391 (ill.); *CWPS:* 265, 282

Afghanistan and *CWA2:* 335–36, 337; *CWB1:* 50, 70, 78; *CWB2:* 393

Africa and *CWA2:* 325–27

African Americans and *CWB1:* 71, 73

as author *CWB1:* 79–80

Brezhnev, Leonid, and *CWA2:* 316, 330; *CWB1:* 49, 50, 74–75

Brown, Harold, and *CWA2:* 321

Brzezinski, Zbigniew, and *CWA2:* 321; *CWB1:* 74, 75

Bush, George, and *CWB1:* 55, 81

cabinet of *CWA2:* 321–22

Camp David Accords and *CWA2:* 328–30; *CWB1:* 70, 78–79; *CWB2:* 263

Carter Doctrine and *CWA2:* 336

Central Intelligence Agency and *CWA2:* 322

China and *CWA2:* 301, 327–28, 336; *CWB1:* 39, 70, 77, 120

Clifford, Clark M., and *CWB1:* 109, 114

Clinton, Bill, and *CWB1:* 81

Conference on Security and Cooperation in Europe and *CWB1:* 75

containment and *CWA2:* 327

Democratic Party and *CWB1:* 73

Deng Xiaoping and *CWA2:* 328; *CWB1:* 120

détente and *CWA2:* 322–23, 335–36; *CWB1:* 74–75

dictatorship and *CWA2:* 322–23, 324, 330–31; *CWB1:* 76

discrimination and *CWB1:* 73

early life of *CWB1:* 71–72

economy and *CWB1:* 76–77; *CWB2:* 391

Egypt and *CWA2:* 328–30

election of *CWA2:* 315, 321, 335, 337–38; *CWB1:* 55, 74; *CWB2:* 390, 391–92

elections monitored by *CWB1:* 80–81

energy policy and *CWB1:* 76–77

as farmer *CWB1:* 72, 73

foreign affairs experience of *CWA2:* 321

as governor *CWB1:* 73–74

Great Depression and *CWB1:* 71–72

Gromyko, Andrey, and *CWA2:* 326

Helsinki Accords and *CWB2:* 265

honors for *CWB1:* 81

human rights and *CWA2:* 315–16, 323–25; *CWB1:* 70, 71–72, 75–76, 80–81

Iran and *CWA2:* 334–35

Iran hostage crisis and *CWB1:* 70, 79; *CWB2:* 391

Israel and *CWA2:* 328–30

Kissinger, Henry, and *CWB2:* 266

Latin America and *CWA2:* 324; *CWB1:* 76

"malaise speech" of *CWB1:* 77

military draft and *CWA2:* 336

as naval officer *CWB1:* 72–73

Nicaragua and *CWA2:* 330–31; *CWB1:* 81

North Korea and *CWB1:* 81; *CWB2:* 248

nuclear weapons and *CWA2:* 315, 323, 330, 336, 337; *CWB1:* 49, 70, 74–75, 77–78, 81, 166; *CWB2:* 248, 392

Olympics and *CWB1:* 70, 78

Pahlavi, Mohammed Reza, and *CWB1:* 79

Pakistan and *CWA2:* 336

Palestine and *CWA2:* 328

Panama and *CWA2:* 263; *CWB1:* 77, 81, 125

presidency of *CWB1:* 73–79

Reagan, Ronald, and *CWB2:* 391–92

Rickover, Hyman G., and *CWB1:* 72–73

Sakharov, Andrey, and *CWA2:* 315, 324; *CWB1:* 75

segregation and *CWB1:* 73

South Korea and *CWA2:* 324

Soviet Union and *CWA2:* 335–36; *CWB1:* 50, 70, 74–75, 77–78; *CWB2:* 393

Strategic Arms Limitation Talks (SALT) and *CWA2:* 323, 330, 336; *CWB1:* 49, 70, 77–78, 166; *CWB2:* 392

Third World and *CWA2:* 325

Trilateral Commission and *CWA2:* 321

Vance, Cyrus, and *CWA2:* 321; *CWB1:* 74

Vietnam War and *CWB1:* 76

Carter, Lillian Gordy *CWB1:* 71

Carter, Rosalynn Smith *CWB1:* 72, 73, 80–81

Casey, William *CWA2:* 332–33

Castillo Armas, Carlos *CWA1:* 169, 180

Castro Argiz, Angel *CWB1:* 83

Castro, Fidel *CWB1:* 82 (ill.), **82–91**; *CWA2:* 209 (ill.), 216 (ill.), 227 (ill.); *CWPS:* 232, 233 (ill.), 233–34, 258

Allende, Salvador, and *CWB1:* 20, 22

as author *CWB1:* 91

Bay of Pigs and *CWA2:* 217–18; *CWB1:* 87; *CWB2:* 341

Central Intelligence Agency and *CWB1:* 87, 88

China and *CWB1:* 86

communism and *CWB1:* 86, 88; *CWB2:* 223

Cuban Missile Crisis and *CWA2:* 229; *CWB1:* 88–89, 90

Cuban Revolution and *CWA2:* 208–9, 214–16, 258

De Rivera, José Antonio Primo, and *CWB1:* 84

democracy and *CWB1:* 86

Dominican Republic and *CWA2:* 264

early life of *CWB1:* 83–84

Eastern Bloc and *CWB1:* 86

economy and *CWB1:* 86–87, 88, 91

Eisenhower, Dwight D., and *CWB1:* 87; *CWB2:* 223

Gorbachev, Mikhail, and *CWB1:* 91

imperialism and *CWB1:* 82–83, 87

Khrushchev, Nikita, and *CWA2:* 217; *CWB2:* 223

Martí, José, and *CWB1:* 84

nation building and *CWA1:* 176; *CWB1:* 83, 88

Operation Mongoose and *CWB1:* 88; *CWB2:* 226

Panama and *CWA2:* 263

presidency of *CWB1:* 86–91

reputation of *CWB1:* 87–88

revolution and *CWB1:* 84–85, 143–44

Soviet Union and *CWA2:* 209–10, 217, 258; *CWB1:* 86, 87, 88–89, 91

26th of July Movement and *CWB1:* 85

Castro, Raúl *CWA2:* 219; *CWB1:* 85, 88

Casualties. *See* Death

CCC. *See* Civilian Conservation Corps (CCC)

CDT. *See* Combined Development Trust (CDT)

CDU. *See* Christian Democratic Union (CDU)

Ceausescu, Nicolae *CWA2:* 360

Center for a New Generation *CWB2:* 405–6

Center for International Security and Arms Control *CWB2:* 404

CENTO. *See* Central Treaty Organization (CENTO)

Central American Policy Committee *CWB2:* 266

Central Committee
of Communist Party *CWB1:* 162

Gorbachev, Mikhail, and *CWB1:* 152–53

Khrushchev, Nikita, and *CWB2:* 232

Kosygin, Aleksey, and *CWB2:* 279

Molotov, Vyacheslav, and *CWB2:* 347

Shevardnadze, Eduard, and *CWB2:* 417

Stalin, Joseph, and *CWB2:* 429

Yeltsin, Boris, and *CWB2:* 419

Zhou Enlai and *CWB2:* 465

Central Intelligence Agency (CIA) *CWPS:* 49, 182
Afghanistan and *CWA2:* 340
Allende, Salvador, and *CWB1:* 24
Bay of Pigs and *CWA2:* 217–18, 259
Bush, George, and *CWB1:* 55
Carter, Jimmy, and *CWA2:* 322
Castro, Fidel, and *CWB1:* 87, 88
Chile and *CWA2:* 308
Congo and *CWA2:* 208
Cuba and *CWA2:* 209, 217–18, 259; *CWB1:* 87, 88, 113, 144; *CWB2:* 223
definition of *CWA1:* 126
espionage and *CWA1:* 34, 143, 145–46, 154, 158, 162
Foreign Intelligence Advisory Board and *CWB1:* 113
formation of *CWA1:* 34, 129–30; *CWB1:* 109
Guatemala and *CWB1:* 141
imperialism and *CWA2:* 208, 209, 217–18, 259, 269–70, 308, 322; *CWB1:* 24, 87, 88, 141, 144; *CWB2:* 223, 398
Iran and *CWA2:* 332, 333; *CWB1:* 141
Iran-Contra scandal and *CWA2:* 332
location of *CWA1:* 131
McCarthy, Joseph R., and *CWA1:* 118
moles and *CWA1:* 154
nation building and *CWA1:* 176, 178, 179–80
Nicaragua and *CWB2:* 398
reconnaissance and *CWA1:* 147, 150

Red Scare and *CWA1:* 118
U-2 and *CWA1:* 147
Vietnam War and *CWA2:* 269–70
Watergate scandal and *CWB2:* 363

Central Party *CWB1:* 10
Central Treaty Organization (CENTO) *CWA2:* 204. *See also* Baghdad Pact
CFE. *See* Conventional Forces in Europe (CFE) treaty
Chamberlain, Neville *CWB1:* 27, 103; *CWB2:* 304
Chambers, Whittaker *CWA1:* 101, 112–13, 113–14; *CWPS:* 148
Chamoun, Camille N. *CWA2:* 204
Champagne, Maurice *CWB2:* 383
"The Chance for Peace" *CWPS:* 89, 99–111, 188
Chang Chi-Chung *CWA1:* 40 (ill.); *CWB2:* 468 (ill.)
Charter of Paris *CWA2:* 366; *CWPS:* 317
Chechnya *CWA2:* 375, 375 (ill.); *CWPS:* 323–24
"Checkers Speech" *CWB2:* 356
Checkpoint Charlie *CWA1:* 75–76, 76 (ill.), 76–77; *CWPS:* 227, 231
Cheka. *See* KGB (Soviet secret police)
Chemical warfare *CWA2:* 283–84, 290; *CWPS:* 311
Cheney Award *CWA1:* 66
Cheney, Richard *CWA2:* 356; *CWPS:* 305
Chernenko, Konstantin *CWA2:* 344, 345, 348, 349, 350; *CWB1:* 44, 45, 152; *CWB2:* 395, 417–18; *CWPS:* 283
Chernobyl disaster *CWB1:* 153

Chiang Ching-kou *CWB1:* 98, 99
Chiang Kai-shek *CWA1:* 40 (ill.); *CWB1:* 92 (ill.), **92–99,** 97 (ill.); *CWPS:* 61–62, 64, 66
civil war and *CWA1:* 38, 41
death of *CWB1:* 99
early life of *CWB1:* 92–93
government of *CWA1:* 46, 184; *CWA2:* 205
Ho Chi Minh and *CWB1:* 179
Japan and *CWB1:* 94–96
Korean War and *CWB1:* 98
Nationalists and *CWB1:* 93–97; *CWB2:* 465, 466, 467
New Life Movement of *CWB1:* 94
popularity of *CWB1:* 39, 96
religion and *CWB1:* 92, 94
Republic of China and *CWB1:* 92, 97–99, 118; *CWB2:* 467
revolution and *CWB1:* 92, 93–97, 117; *CWB2:* 298–99, 315–16, 324, 465, 466, 467
Soviet Union and *CWB1:* 93
Sun Yat-sen and *CWB1:* 93
Truman, Harry S., and *CWB1:* 96, 98
United Front and *CWB1:* 96
World War II and *CWB1:* 96
Zhou Enlai and *CWB1:* 94–96
Chiang Kai-shek, Madame *CWB1:* 94, 95, 95 (ill.)
Chief Intelligence Directorate of the General Staff of the Red Army. *See* GRU (Soviet military intelligence agency)

nuclear weapons and *CWA1:* 185; *CWA2:* 206, 246–47, 258, 266, 300, 373; *CWB2:* 318

peace and *CWPS:* 277–78, 279

perestroika and *CWB1:* 121

press and *CWPS:* 276

Red Army in *CWB2:* 316, 466

Red Guard in *CWA2:* 266, 267 (ill.), 294, 295, 295 (ill.); *CWB2:* 318, 472

Red Scare and *CWA1:* 111; *CWB2:* 333

revolution in *CWB1:* 5–6, 39, 92, 93–97, 117; *CWB2:* 243, 298–99, 313, 315–16, 324, 464–67; *CWPS:* 61–62, 64–70

Rusk, Dean, and *CWB1:* 202

Sian Incident in *CWB1:* 94–96

Sino-Soviet Treaty and *CWB2:* 316–17; *CWPS:* 69

Soviet Union and *CWA1:* 40–42, 52, 111, 184–85; *CWA2:* 205–6, 265–66, 300–301, 301–2, 327, 356; *CWB1:* 47, 93, 116, 118; *CWB2:* 235, 280, 316–18, 471; *CWPS:* 65, 68, 69, 70, 264, 274, 294

Stalin, Joseph, and *CWA1:* 40, 42; *CWB2:* 317; *CWPS:* 65, 70

Taiwan and *CWA1:* 50, 183–85; *CWA2:* 205, 266, 301; *CWB1:* 98–99, 130; *CWB2:* 469

Tiananmen Square *CWA2:* 295 (ill.), 362; *CWB1:* 121; *CWB2:* 314

Truman, Harry S., and *CWA1:* 40, 42; *CWB1:* 96, 98, 139; *CWB2:*

298, 324, 467; *CWPS:* 62, 65, 67–68, 101

United Front in *CWB1:* 96

United Nations and *CWA2:* 266, 327; *CWB1:* 98–99, 119; *CWB2:* 313, 360, 469

U.S. State Department and *CWPS:* 65, 67–68

Vietnam and *CWA1:* 42; *CWA2:* 328; *CWB2:* 469

Vietnam War and *CWA2:* 270–71, 290, 301; *CWPS:* 267, 272, 274–76

World War II and *CWA1:* 12, 39; *CWB1:* 96; *CWB2:* 316

China Lobby *CWB1:* 95, 98; *CWB2:* 360, 469; *CWPS:* 62, 65

Chisholm, Janet *CWA1:* 152

Chou Enlai *CWA1:* 176, 184

Christian Democratic Union (CDU) *CWB1:* 11, 14–15; *CWB2:* 270, 271, 274

Christmas bombing *CWA2:* 313; *CWB2:* 259, 359

Chu Teh *CWB2:* 468 (ill.)

Churchill, Winston *CWA1:* 14 (ill.), 30 (ill.); *CWB1:* 100 (ill.), **100–108**; *CWB2:* 457 (ill.); *CWPS:* 17 (ill.), 19 (ill.), 22 (ill.)

Attlee, Clement R., and *CWB1:* 27–28

as author *CWB1:* 102, 103

Bevin, Ernest, and *CWB1:* 35

Big Three and *CWA1:* 2, 9–10, 29; *CWB1:* 104–6

communism and *CWB1:* 100, 107

death of *CWB1:* 108

early life of *CWB1:* 101–2

elections and *CWA1:* 15, 171; *CWB1:* 27, 32, 40, 107; *CWB2:* 304, 305; *CWPS:* 16

Elizabeth II and *CWB1:* 100–101

espionage and *CWA1:* 140, 142

Harriman, W. Averell, and *CWB1:* 171

Hitler, Adolf, and *CWB1:* 102–3, 104

honors for *CWB1:* 100–101, 103

Iron Curtain and *CWA1:* 20–21; *CWB1:* 100, 107

"Iron Curtain speech" and *CWPS:* 4, 12–13, **16–24**, 25, 26, 28–29

as journalist *CWB1:* 101–2

Kennedy, John F., and *CWB1:* 101

Macmillan, Harold, and *CWB2:* 304–5

military and *CWB1:* 101

Molotov, Vyacheslav, and *CWB2:* 349

nuclear weapons and *CWA1:* 171; *CWB1:* 31, 108

peace and *CWPS:* 110

politics and *CWB1:* 102

Potsdam Conference and *CWB1:* 35–36; *CWB2:* 431

retirement of *CWB1:* 108

Roosevelt, Franklin D., and *CWB1:* 105–6; *CWB2:* 431

Soviet Union and *CWB1:* 108

Stalin, Joseph, and *CWB1:* 105–6, 107; *CWB2:* 431; *CWPS:* 19, 23

Tehran Conference and *CWB2:* 431

Truman, Harry S., and *CWB1:* 107–8; *CWB2:* 457; *CWPS:* 12, 16

United Nations and *CWA1:* 12

World War I and *CWB1:* 102; *CWPS:* 20

World War II and *CWB1:* 27–28, 100, 102–6;

CWB2: 304–5, 349; *CWPS:* 16–17, 21

Yalta agreements and *CWA1:* 2, 10, 11, 105; *CWB1:* 65, 66; *CWB2:* 431

Yalta Conference and *CWPS:* 18

CIA. *See* Central Intelligence Agency (CIA)

Ciphers
Cambridge Spies and *CWA1:* 142
SIGINT and *CWA2:* 224
tradecraft and *CWA1:* 137
U.S. Navy and *CWA1:* 155–57
VENONA and *CWA1:* 127, 132–35
World War II and *CWA1:* 131

CIS. *See* Commonwealth of Independent States (CIS)

Civil Defense *CWPS:* 212–13, 215

Civil rights *CWPS:* 127, 133, 142. *See also* Freedom; Human rights
Allende, Salvador, and *CWB1:* 23
Civil Rights Act of 1964 *CWA2:* 254, 282
communism and *CWB2:* 385
democracy and *CWB2:* 385
Federal Bureau of Investigation and *CWB1:* 187, 193
Hoover, J. Edgar, and *CWA1:* 109
House Un-American Activities Committee and *CWB2:* 333
Johnson, Lyndon B., and *CWB1:* 194, 196, 197, 198; *CWB2:* 222
Kennedy, John F., and *CWB2:* 218, 221–22
loyalty programs and *CWA1:* 107

McCarthy, Joseph R., and *CWB2:* 336

Nixon, Richard M., and *CWB2:* 357, 358–59

Red Scare and *CWA1:* 110, 113, 115, 172; *CWB2:* 333

Rice, Condoleezza, and *CWB2:* 402–3

Civil Rights Act of 1957 *CWB1:* 196

Civil Rights Act of 1964 *CWA2:* 254, 282; *CWB1:* 194, 197; *CWB2:* 222

Civilian Conservation Corps (CCC) *CWB2:* 295, 323

Clark, Tom Campbell *CWA1:* 107

Clausewitz, Karl von *CWPS:* 192

Clayton, Will *CWPS:* 43

Cleaver, Eldridge *CWA2:* 281

Clegg, Hugh *CWA1:* 138 (ill.)

Clifford, Clark M. *CWA1:* 22; *CWA2:* 273; *CWB1:* 109 (ill.), **109–15,** 112 (ill.)

Clifford-Elsey Report *CWB1:* 110–11

Clifton, Chester *CWA1:* 72; *CWPS:* 226

Clinton, Bill *CWB1:* 60, 81; *CWB2:* 364, 403; *CWPS:* 324, 325

Cloaks *CWA1:* 141

Closed societies *CWPS:* 4

CND. *See* Campaign for Nuclear Disarmament (CND)

Coal *CWA1:* 64, 65, 65 (ill.)

Cohn, Roy *CWA1:* 118; *CWB2:* 334; *CWPS:* 167 (ill.)

Cold War *CWA1:* 106 (ill.)
balance in *CWA1:* 169; *CWA2:* 374
beginning of *CWA1:* 1–3, 20, 23–24; *CWB1:* 172; *CWB2:* 212; *CWPS:* 1–4

Berlin airlift and *CWA1:* 66

capitalism and *CWA1:* 25, 60; *CWB2:* 384–85

causes of *CWA1:* 23–24, 29

colonialism and *CWB1:* 180

communism and *CWA1:* 25, 60, 105; *CWB2:* 316–17, 384–85

costs of *CWA2:* 372–73; *CWPS:* 324

death in *CWA2:* 372

definition of *CWA1:* 1–2, 28, 56, 80, 100, 126, 168; *CWA2:* 192, 234, 252, 276, 298, 320, 348

democracy and *CWA1:* 25, 60, 105; *CWA2:* 347; *CWB2:* 316–17

description of *CWB1:* 42, 190

détente and *CWA2:* 297–300

economy and *CWA1:* 24–25

Eisenhower, Dwight D., and *CWA1:* 52

end of *CWA1:* 66, 160; *CWA2:* 347, 351, 355, 357, 370–72; *CWB1:* 58; *CWB2:* 265, 274, 421; *CWPS:* 293–97, 319–25

espionage and *CWA1:* 24, 127–29, 129–32

fear and *CWA1:* 105, 128–29; *CWPS:* 185, 186, 198

freedom and *CWA2:* 347

Germany and *CWA1:* 60–61

Japan and *CWB2:* 298

Kennan, George F., on *CWB2:* 396

Khrushchev, Nikita, and *CWA1:* 52

Khrushchev, Sergei, on *CWPS:* 185–86, 192–93

as Long Peace *CWA2:* 374

Macmillan, Harold, and *CWB2:* 303

name of *CWA1:* 2–3

Nixon, Richard M., and *CWB2:* 354

nuclear weapons and *CWA2:* 233–35; *CWB2:* 366–67; *CWPS:* 192–93

origins of *CWA1:* 3–25

peace and *CWA2:* 374

Reagan, Ronald, and *CWB2:* 387, 396

Red Scare and *CWA1:* 114

Shevardnadze, Eduard, and *CWB2:* 416

Stalin, Joseph, and *CWA1:* 25, 52

thaw of *CWA1:* 187–88; *CWA2:* 192–93, 297–300

Truman, Harry S., and *CWA1:* 24, 25, 52; *CWB2:* 452, 458–59, 459–61, 462

Collectivism *CWB2:* 384, 409, 429, 448

Colombo Plan *CWB1:* 40

Colonialism *CWB1:* 177–79, 180; *CWB2:* 309–10. *See also* Imperialism

Africa and *CWA2:* 206–8

containment and *CWA2:* 206

France and *CWA2:* 206, 268–69

Great Britain and *CWA2:* 202, 206

Indochina and *CWA2:* 268–69

Middle East and *CWA2:* 202

Monroe Doctrine and *CWA1:* 186–87

nation building and *CWA1:* 176–78

Portugal and *CWA2:* 206

Combined Airlift Task Force *CWA1:* 65

Combined Development Trust (CDT) *CWA1:* 143

Combined Policy Committee (CPC) *CWA1:* 143

Comecon. *See* Council of Mutual Economic Assistance (Comecon)

Cominform. *See* Communist Information Bureau (Cominform)

Comintern *CWB2:* 412, 446; *CWPS:* 19

Committee for State Security. *See* KGB (Soviet secret police)

Committee of 100 *CWA2:* 245–46

Committee on the Present Danger *CWA2:* 338

Committee to Reelect the President (CREEP) *CWA2:* 310

Common Market *CWB1:* 14; *CWB2:* 308–9

Commonwealth of Independent States (CIS) *CWA2:* 370, 374–76; *CWB2:* 423; *CWPS:* 296. *See also* Russia; Soviet Union

"Communiqué to President Kennedy Accepting an End to the Missile Crisis, October 28, 1962" *CWPS:* 253–62

Communism. *See also* Collectivism; Communist Party

Acheson, Dean G., and *CWPS:* 35–36

Asia and *CWPS:* 211

in Berlin *CWA1:* 57, 73

Berlin Wall and *CWB2:* 226

Bolshevik Revolution and *CWA1:* 2, 3–5, 6–7; *CWB1:* 187; *CWB2:* 231, 380–81

capitalism and *CWA1:* 19, 23–24, 25, 29, 33, 129, 169–70, 188; *CWA2:* 215–16, 352; *CWB1:* 111, 150, 181, 186; *CWB2:* 210–11, 237, 251, 272, 351, 357, 385, 433–34; *CWPS:* 5, 11, 48, 99, 128, 148, 149, 301–2, 305

Castro, Fidel, and *CWB1:* 86, 88; *CWB2:* 223

Chiang Kai-shek, Madame, and *CWB1:* 95

in China *CWB1:* 93–97, 117–23; *CWB2:* 235, 312, 314–15, 317–18, 319, 360, 434; *CWPS:* 62, 64–70

Churchill, Winston, and *CWB1:* 100, 107

civil rights and *CWB2:* 385

Clifford, Clark M., and *CWB1:* 110–11

closed societies and *CWPS:* 4

Cold War and *CWA1:* 25, 60, 105; *CWB2:* 316–17, 384–85

collapse of *CWA2:* 347, 357–60; *CWB1:* 53, 57–59, 122; *CWB2:* 273–74, 396, 405, 421–22, 442; *CWPS:* 295–97, 307, 309, 315

Comintern and *CWPS:* 19

Communist Party and *CWB1:* 17–18, 26, 42, 82, 100, 110, 127, 159–60, 162, 168, 178, 186; *CWB2:* 223, 231, 251, 278, 312, 340, 346, 366, 385, 410, 426, 445; *CWPS:* 1, 150

in Cuba *CWA2:* 216–17; *CWB1:* 82, 88

Cultural Revolution and *CWA2:* 277, 293–94

in Czechoslovakia *CWPS:* 50, 53, 54, 56, 67

definition of *CWA1:* 2, 28, 56, 80, 99, 100, 126, 168; *CWA2:* 192, 214, 234, 252, 276, 298, 320, 348; *CWB1:* 17–18

democracy and *CWA1:* 100–101, 128–29, 167–68; *CWA2:* 215–16, 267–68, 319, 347; *CWB1:* 168, 186, 189; *CWB2:* 251, 316–17, 366, 404; *CWPS:* 26, 36, 123, 124, 127, 128,

348; *CWB1:* 3, 18, 26, 42, 82, 100, 110, 127, 150, 160, 168, 178, 186; *CWB2:* 211, 223, 231, 278, 295, 312, 331, 340, 346, 366, 385, 389, 404, 410, 426, 445, 458, 464; *CWPS:* 1–2, 150, 204

racism and *CWPS:* 152

Rand, Ayn, and *CWB2:* 379, 381, 384

Reagan, Ronald, and *CWA2:* 338; *CWB2:* 251, 387, 389; *CWPS:* 124, 135, 139–42, 282, 284–85

Red Scare and *CWB2:* 332–33, 376, 389

religion and *CWA1:* 2, 3, 28, 56, 80, 99, 100, 126, 128, 167, 168; *CWA2:* 192, 214, 234, 252, 276, 292, 298, 320, 348; *CWB2:* 385, 389; *CWPS:* 2, 132, 138, 151, 152, 168, 284–85

Rice, Condoleezza, and *CWB2:* 404

Roosevelt, Eleanor, and *CWPS:* 91, 95

Roosevelt, Franklin D., and *CWB1:* 185–86, 189; *CWPS:* 125

Rosenberg, Ethel, and *CWA1:* 139

Rosenberg, Julius, and *CWA1:* 139

Rusk, Dean, and *CWB1:* 201, 202

school and *CWPS:* 149–50, 151, 163

socialism and *CWPS:* 128

in Soviet Union *CWA1:* 27–29; *CWA2:* 299; *CWB1:* 26, 110, 127; *CWB2:* 385, 410, 418; *CWPS:* 5–14, 72, 73–76, 168–70

Stalin, Joseph, and *CWB2:* 236, 426–28, 433–34; *CWPS:* 2

teachers and *CWA1:* 115

in Third World *CWA1:* 176–78; *CWA2:* 193

Tito, Josip Broz, and *CWB2:* 445–46

travel and *CWPS:* 151

Truman Doctrine and *CWB1:* 3–4

in Turkey *CWPS:* 32–33, 34–41

United Nations and *CWPS:* 88, 90, 91, 94, 95

U.S. Congress and *CWPS:* 162, 170–71

in Vietnam *CWA1:* 42

Vietnam War and *CWA2:* 283, 284, 290

West Berlin and *CWPS:* 210

in Yugoslavia *CWA1:* 51

Zhou Enlai and *CWB2:* 464

Communist fronts *CWPS:* 157–58

Communist Information Bureau (Cominform) *CWA1:* 33; *CWB2:* 434, 448; *CWPS:* 11, 45, 161

Communist Party. *See also* Communism

Allende, Salvador, and *CWB1:* 18, 19

Andropov, Yuri, and *CWB2:* 417

Beria, Lavrenty, and *CWB2:* 433

Bolshevik Revolution and *CWA1:* 2, 4–5; *CWB1:* 45

Brezhnev, Leonid, and *CWB1:* 41, 42, 43–46, 49–50

Central Committee of *CWB1:* 152–53, 162; *CWB2:* 232, 279, 347, 417, 419, 429, 465

Chernenko, Konstantin, and *CWB1:* 45; *CWB2:* 417

in Chile *CWB1:* 19

in China *CWA1:* 38–42, 111; *CWA2:* 294–95; *CWB2:* 313, 315, 317, 318, 465–66, 467

communism and *CWB1:* 17–18, 26, 42, 82, 100, 110, 127, 159–60, 162, 168, 178, 186; *CWB2:* 223, 231, 251, 278, 312, 340, 346, 366, 385, 410, 426, 445; *CWPS:* 1, 150

Council of Ministers in *CWB1:* 162, 163, 166; *CWB2:* 240, 277, 279, 280, 282

coup attempt by *CWA2:* 368–69; *CWPS:* 320

in Cuba *CWB1:* 86

Cultural Revolution and *CWA2:* 294–95

in Czechoslovakia *CWA1:* 32, 34–35, 37; *CWA2:* 359–60

democracy and *CWA2:* 267–68

Deng Xiaoping and *CWB1:* 117, 118, 119, 122–23

in East Germany *CWA2:* 358–59

elections and *CWA1:* 27

end of *CWB2:* 422

formation of *CWA1:* 2, 3, 7; *CWB1:* 159

in France *CWA1:* 31; *CWB1:* 178

freedom and *CWB2:* 434; *CWPS:* 299

fronts for *CWPS:* 157–58

Gorbachev, Mikhail, and *CWA2:* 347, 360–62, 367–68, 372; *CWB1:* 146, 150, 151, 152–53, 153–54, 157, 166; *CWB2:* 418, 419; *CWPS:* 296, 315

Great Terror and *CWB1:* 45

Gromyko, Andrey, and *CWB1:* 162–63, 165, 166–67

Ho Chi Minh and *CWB1:* 178, 179

in Hungary *CWA2:* 358

in Indochina *CWB1:* 179

in Italy *CWA1:* 31

Khrushchev, Nikita, and *CWA1:* 170, 188; *CWA2:* 241, 254–55, 260; *CWB2:* 231–32, 233, 234, 240; *CWPS:* 174–75, 176–77, 181–82

Kosygin, Aleksey, and *CWB1:* 46; *CWB2:* 277, 278–79, 279–80, 282

Lenin, Vladimir I., and *CWA1:* 3, 101; *CWB1:* 159; *CWPS:* 2

Mao Zedong and *CWB2:* 313, 315, 317, 318, 467

Molotov, Vyacheslav, and *CWB2:* 347, 353

Podgorny, Nikolay, and *CWB1:* 46

in Poland *CWA1:* 11, 12–13; *CWA2:* 357–58

Politburo in *CWB1:* 118, 152, 162–63, 165; *CWB2:* 232, 234, 240, 279, 280, 347, 352, 418, 465–66; *CWPS:* 11, 174, 283

Presidium in *CWB1:* 44, 163; *CWB2:* 419

in Romania *CWA2:* 360

in Russia *CWA1:* 3, 101; *CWA2:* 369, 373

Sakharov, Andrey, and *CWB2:* 410

Secretariat of *CWB1:* 162

Shevardnadze, Eduard, and *CWB2:* 417

in Soviet Union *CWA1:* 120, 121, 170, 188; *CWA2:* 241, 254–55, 260, 338, 347, 348–49, 360–62, 367–69, 372; *CWB1:* 41, 42, 43–46, 49–50, 153–54, 157, 162–63; *CWB2:* 231–32, 233, 234, 239–40, 277, 278–79, 279–80, 347, 353, 410, 417–18, 419, 429, 430, 433; *CWPS:* 174–75, 176–77, 181–82, 296, 315

Stalin, Joseph, and *CWA1:* 120, 121; *CWB2:* 429, 430

structure of *CWB1:* 162–63

Taiwan and *CWA1:* 184–85

Tito, Josip Broz, and *CWB2:* 445–46

in United States of America *CWB1:* 192; *CWPS:* 153–57, 159–61

in Vietnam *CWB1:* 176

Yeltsin, Boris, and *CWA2:* 369; *CWB1:* 157; *CWB2:* 419

in Yugoslavia *CWB2:* 445–46

Zhou Enlai and *CWB2:* 465–66

Conant, James B. *CWB2:* 375

Conference on Security and Cooperation in Europe (CSCE) *CWA2:* 348, 365–66; *CWB1:* 75; *CWB2:* 264–65; *CWPS:* 48

Confucianism *CWB1:* 92, 177

Congo *CWA2:* 207–8, 326–27

Congress of People's Deputies *CWA2:* 360–61; *CWB1:* 154, 157; *CWB2:* 414–15; *CWPS:* 304–5

Congressional Medal of Honor *CWB2:* 296–97

Conkin, Paul K. *CWB1:* 194

Connally, John B. *CWB2:* 228

Conservative Party *CWA1:* 15

in Great Britain *CWB1:* 25, 27, 102; *CWB2:* 443

Macmillan, Harold, and *CWB2:* 304

Thatcher, Margaret, and *CWB2:* 439

Containment

Africa and *CWA2:* 325–27

Asia and *CWPS:* 62, 65–66, 67–68, 81, 264

Attlee, Clement R., and *CWB1:* 30–32

Carter, Jimmy, and *CWA2:* 327

China and *CWPS:* 65–66, 67–68, 81

Clifford, Clark M., and *CWB1:* 111

Colombo Plan and *CWB1:* 40

colonialism and *CWA2:* 206

definition of *CWA1:* 28

diplomacy and *CWPS:* 9, 14, 72, 75

Dulles, John Foster, and *CWB1:* 128

economy and *CWA1:* 28, 31–32, 35–36, 49–50, 51; *CWPS:* 9, 44, 52–59, 61, 75

Eisenhower Doctrine and *CWB1:* 132, 142

Eisenhower, Dwight D., and *CWA2:* 202; *CWB1:* 141, 142

Four Point Program and *CWA1:* 49–50

Germany and *CWA1:* 58; *CWB2:* 432

Harriman, W. Averell, and *CWB1:* 168, 171–72

Iran and *CWA2:* 334

Japan and *CWB1:* 128; *CWB2:* 298

Johnson, Lyndon B., and *CWB1:* 198; *CWPS:* 263–64

Kennan, George F., and *CWA1:* 35–36; *CWB2:* 207, 212–13; *CWPS:* 4, 9, 13, 14, 62, 72

Kennedy, John F., and *CWPS:* 263

Kohl, Helmut, and *CWB2:* 272–73

Korean War and *CWA1:* 46

"Long Telegram" and *CWPS:* 3–4

MacArthur, Douglas, and *CWB2:* 295, 297, 298, 299; *CWPS:* 81, 82–84

Marshall, George C., and *CWB2:* 325

Marshall Plan and *CWA1:* 31–32; *CWB1:* 112–13, 172; *CWPS:* 9, 44, 52–59, 61

Middle East and *CWA2:* 202

military and *CWA1:* 36, 44–45, 48–49, 50; *CWB2:* 213; *CWPS:* 9, 14, 72, 74–78, 119

National Security Council (NSC) and *CWA1:* 28, 32, 44–45; *CWPS:* 62, 72, 74–77

Nitze, Paul H., and *CWPS:* 62, 72, 74–77

Nixon Doctrine and *CWPS:* 264, 268–73

Nixon, Richard M., and *CWPS:* 264, 268–73

North Atlantic Treaty Organization (NATO) and *CWA1:* 28, 168; *CWA2:* 348; *CWB1:* 4, 31, 58, 111, 113; *CWB2:* 271, 327, 434, 437

NSC-68 and *CWA1:* 28, 44–45

nuclear weapons and *CWA1:* 32, 92, 93; *CWB2:* 272–73; *CWPS:* 9, 14

politics and *CWA1:* 36; *CWB2:* 213; *CWPS:* 9, 14

Reagan, Ronald, and *CWA2:* 340–41; *CWB2:* 395–97

Rio Pact and *CWA1:* 36

Southeast Asia Treaty Organization (SEATO) and *CWA1:* 168; *CWB1:* 130, 141

Stalin, Joseph, and *CWB2:* 433–34

strength and *CWA1:* 93

Truman Doctrine and *CWB1:* 3–4, 29–30, 38, 112, 172; *CWPS:* 33

Truman, Harry S., and *CWA1:* 29–30, 168–69, 173–74; *CWB1:* 3–4, 29–30, 38, 128, 172;

CWB2: 458–59; *CWPS:* 33, 52–59, 62

Contras *CWA2:* 331–32, 332–33; *CWB1:* 56; *CWB2:* 398

Conventional Forces in Europe (CFE) treaty *CWA2:* 355, 365–66; *CWB2:* 274

CORONA *CWA1:* 150

Council of Foreign Ministers *CWA1:* 17–18

Council of Ministers
in Communist Party *CWB1:* 162, 163
Gromyko, Andrey, and *CWB1:* 166
Khrushchev, Nikita, and *CWB2:* 240
Kosygin, Aleksey, and *CWB2:* 277, 279, 280, 282

Council of Mutual Economic Assistance (Comecon) *CWA1:* 33–34; *CWPS:* 45

Council on Foreign Relations *CWB2:* 256

Counterculture *CWA2:* 276, 286–88

Counterintelligence *CWA1:* 125, 126

Country Joe and the Fish *CWA2:* 288

Country wall *CWA1:* 74. *See also* Berlin Wall

Cox, Edward *CWA2:* 311 (ill.)

Cox, Tricia *CWA2:* 311 (ill.)

CPC. *See* Combined Policy Committee (CPC)

CREEP. *See* Committee to Reelect the President (CREEP)

"Crimes of Stalin speech" *CWA1:* 188; *CWA2:* 192–93; *CWB2:* 236, 291, 436; *CWPS:* 175, **176–83**

Cruise missiles *CWA2:* 330

Crusade in Europe CWB1: 139; *CWPS:* 100

CSCE. *See* Conference on Security and Cooperation in Europe (CSCE)

Cuba *CWA2:* 218 (ill.), 220 (ill.), 223; *CWPS:* 232, 233–34, 256–57, 259, 263. *See also* Cuban Missile Crisis
agriculture in *CWB1:* 86
Bay of Pigs *CWA2:* 214, 217–18, 218 (ill.), 252, 258–59; *CWB1:* 87, 113, 144; *CWB2:* 223, 340–41
blockade of *CWB1:* 90; *CWB2:* 227, 238
Central Intelligence Agency (CIA) and *CWA2:* 209, 217–18, 259; *CWB1:* 87, 88, 113, 144; *CWB2:* 223
China and *CWB1:* 86
communism in *CWA2:* 216–17; *CWB1:* 82, 88
Communist Party in *CWB1:* 86
Cuban Missile Crisis and *CWB1:* 88–91
Cuban People's Party in *CWB1:* 84–85
Czechoslovakia and *CWA2:* 221
democracy in *CWB1:* 86
dictatorship and *CWA2:* 208, 215; *CWB1:* 84–85
Eastern Bloc and *CWB1:* 86
economy of *CWA2:* 208, 209–10, 215, 216–17; *CWB1:* 84–85, 86–87, 88, 91
Eisenhower, Dwight D., and *CWA2:* 208–10, 216–17, 258; *CWB1:* 87, 143–44; *CWB2:* 223
elections in *CWA2:* 216
Gorbachev, Mikhail, and *CWB1:* 91
imperialism and *CWA2:* 217–19
Kennedy, John F., and *CWB1:* 87, 88

nation building and *CWA1:* 180

nationalization in *CWB1:* 86

nuclear weapons and *CWA2:* 219–20, 248, 265; *CWB1:* 88–91

Operation Mongoose and *CWA2:* 219

revolution in *CWA2:* 208–9, 214–16, 258; *CWB1:* 84–85, 143–44

Soviet Union and *CWA2:* 209–10, 216, 217, 219–21, 258, 273, 310; *CWB1:* 82, 86, 87, 88–91; *CWB2:* 223, 226–27

Spain and *CWB1:* 83

submarine base in *CWA2:* 310

26th of July Movement and *CWB1:* 85

United Nations and *CWB1:* 91

Cuban Missile Crisis *CWA2:* 220 (ill.), 223 (ill.), 227 (ill.); *CWB1:* 89 (ill.); *CWPS:* 237 (ill.), 250 (ill.), 254 (ill.), 257 (ill.)

Acheson, Dean G., and *CWB1:* 7

anniversary of *CWPS:* 258–59

announcement of *CWA2:* 226–27

Black Saturday *CWA2:* 228; *CWPS:* 255

blockade and *CWA2:* 214, 225–26, 227–29, 260; *CWB1:* 90; *CWB2:* 227, 238; *CWPS:* 237, 238, 241, 244, 247, 249–50, 253

Bundy, McGeorge, and *CWPS:* 236

Castro, Fidel, and *CWB1:* 88–89, 90

DEFCON and *CWPS:* 253, 260–61

definition of *CWA2:* 214, 252

Dobrynin, Anatoly, and *CWPS:* 253–55

Ex-Comm and *CWA2:* 221–25; *CWPS:* 234, 236–37, 238–43

installation of missiles *CWA2:* 219–20, 260

intelligence and *CWA1:* 150; *CWA2:* 221–25, 223 (ill.), 260; *CWPS:* 237, 250

Kennedy, John F., and *CWA2:* 213–14, 221–27, 228, 229, 260; *CWB1:* 7, 89–91; *CWB2:* 218, 226–28, 238, 308; *CWPS:* 192, 234–35, 236–37, 238–39, 241–42, 244–51, 253–61

Kennedy, Robert F., and *CWB2:* 227; *CWPS:* 234, 236–43, 253–55

Khrushchev, Nikita, and *CWA2:* 219–20, 226, 227, 228, 229, 260; *CWB1:* 90–91; *CWB2:* 226–27, 227–28, 230, 238; *CWPS:* 192, 234, 235, 244–45, 248–50, 251–62

Khrushchev, Sergei, on *CWPS:* 250, 256

Kosygin, Aleksey, and *CWB2:* 277

Macmillan, Harold, and *CWB2:* 308

McNamara, Robert S., and *CWPS:* 241, 242, 259

military and *CWPS:* 241, 248, 253, 260–61

missiles and *CWPS:* 234, 236, 237–38, 244, 246–47, 251

National Security Agency (NSA) and *CWA2:* 221, 224

National Security Council (NSC) and *CWA2:* 221–25; *CWPS:* 234, 236

negotiations concerning *CWA2:* 228–29, 260

nuclear war and *CWA2:* 213–14, 222, 226–28, 230, 239, 241, 252, 254, 372; *CWB2:* 227, 238, 394; *CWPS:* 235, 238, 246–47, 253, 256, 259, 260, 261

nuclear weapons and *CWB1:* 88–91; *CWPS:* 121, 234, 238, 242–43, 244, 246–47, 248, 256

Organization of American States (OAS) and *CWA2:* 226; *CWPS:* 241, 248

peace and *CWPS:* 246–47, 248–49, 256, 258, 260

press and *CWPS:* 261

reconnaissance and *CWB1:* 90; *CWB2:* 227; *CWPS:* 236, 246, 247, 255

Rusk, Dean, and *CWPS:* 250

SIGINT and *CWPS:* 234, 250

Soviet Union and *CWPS:* 246–49

Strategic Air Command (SAC) and *CWA2:* 225

Turkey and *CWA2:* 228, 229–30, 260; *CWPS:* 234, 255

United Nations and *CWA2:* 226, 227; *CWPS:* 241, 248, 249

U.S. Air Force and *CWA2:* 225

Cuban People's Party *CWB1:* 84–85

Cultural Revolution *CWA2:* 266–67, 276, 277, 293–95, 295 (ill.); *CWB1:* 119; *CWB2:* 246, 318–20, 471–72

Culture *CWA2:* 276, 286–88, 292–93, 338; *CWPS:* 278, 280

Cummings, Homer S. *CWB1:* 190 (ill.)

Currency *CWA1:* 62

Czech National Committee *CWA1:* 34

Czechoslovakia *CWA2:* 359 (ill.)
Brezhnev, Leonid, and *CWB1:* 43, 47; *CWB2:* 282
communism in *CWPS:* 50, 53, 54, 56, 67
Communist Party in *CWA1:* 32, 34–35, 37; *CWA2:* 359–60
Cuba and *CWA2:* 221
Czech National Committee and *CWA1:* 34
democracy and *CWA2:* 359–60
economy of *CWA2:* 267
Egypt and *CWA2:* 202
elections in *CWA2:* 360
freedom in *CWB1:* 47
Germany and *CWA1:* 34
Gromyko, Andrey, and *CWB1:* 164
Mao Zedong and *CWA2:* 300
Marshall Plan and *CWA1:* 34; *CWPS:* 48, 50
Prague Spring and *CWA2:* 252, 267–68
Soviet Union and *CWA1:* 34; *CWA2:* 268; *CWB1:* 43, 47, 164, 204; *CWB2:* 216, 281, 282, 449
Sovietization of *CWB1:* 43
Stalin, Joseph, and *CWB2:* 435
Warsaw Pact and *CWA2:* 268
Yugoslavia and *CWB2:* 449

D

Dag Hammarskjold Honorary Medal *CWB2:* 343
Daggers *CWA1:* 141
Daily Worker CWPS: 128
Davidenko, Viktor *CWA1:* 95
Davies, Joseph *CWB2:* 209–10

De Gaulle, Charles *CWA2:* 299, 306; *CWB1:* 14; *CWB2:* 305, 308, 309
De Rivera, José Antonio Primo *CWB1:* 84
Dead drops *CWA1:* 136, 152
Death *CWPS:* 267–68, 324. *See also* Execution
Berlin airlift and *CWA1:* 63
Berlin Wall and *CWA1:* 74
in Cold War *CWA2:* 372
in Cultural Revolution *CWB2:* 318, 320
in Great Terror *CWA1:* 120, 121, 123; *CWB1:* 42–43; *CWB2:* 232, 236, 278, 370, 412, 430, 434–35
in Korean War *CWA1:* 48; *CWA2:* 372
Stalin, Joseph, on *CWB2:* 425
in Vietnam War *CWA2:* 271, 273, 283–84, 290, 313, 372; *CWB1:* 201; *CWB2:* 258, 359
in World War II *CWA1:* 17, 57, 87–88; *CWB2:* 458
DeBakey, Michael *CWB2:* 419
Declaration of Human Rights *CWA2:* 315
Declaration on Liberated Europe *CWA1:* 9
DEFCON *CWA2:* 226–27, 227–28, 229, 241; *CWPS:* 253, 260–61
Defection *CWA1:* 163–64
Defense Condition. *See* DEFCON
"The Demands of the Annamite People" *CWB1:* 178
Demilitarized Zone (DMZ) *CWB2:* 244
DeMille, Cecil B. *CWB2:* 382–83
Democracy
Allende, Salvador, and *CWB1:* 17

Bonner, Yelena, and *CWB2:* 415
Bush, George, and *CWA2:* 369
capitalism and *CWA2:* 299, 320; *CWB1:* 42
Castro, Fidel, and *CWB1:* 86
China and *CWA2:* 362; *CWB2:* 314
civil rights and *CWB2:* 385
Cold War and *CWA1:* 25, 60, 105; *CWA2:* 347; *CWB2:* 316–17
communism and *CWA1:* 100–101, 128–29, 167–68; *CWA2:* 215–16, 267–68, 319, 347; *CWB1:* 168, 186, 189; *CWB2:* 251, 316–17, 366, 404; *CWPS:* 26, 36, 123, 124, 127, 128, 141, 142, 166, 170, 204, 289
Communist Party and *CWA2:* 267–68
Conference on Security and Cooperation in Europe and *CWB2:* 265
in Cuba *CWB1:* 86
Czechoslovakia and *CWA2:* 359–60
definition of *CWA1:* 4; *CWA2:* 192, 214, 276, 298, 320
East Germany and *CWA2:* 358–59; *CWB2:* 421
Eastern Bloc and *CWA2:* 357–60; *CWPS:* 54, 56
economy and *CWA2:* 262; *CWB2:* 426
elections and *CWA1:* 4, 27, 58, 128, 167–68; *CWA2:* 192, 214, 216, 276, 298, 299, 320; *CWB1:* 25–26, 42, 86, 127; *CWB2:* 251, 271, 314, 385, 404, 426, 449; *CWPS:* 1
Europe and *CWPS:* 2–3
facism and *CWB1:* 186, 189

Watergate scandal and *CWA2:* 299, 310–11; *CWB2:* 264

West Berlin and *CWA2:* 306

Deterrence *CWPS:* 53

Dewey, Thomas *CWB1:* 127–28; *CWB2:* 459, 460

Dictatorship
capitalism and *CWB1:* 84–85, 99

Carter, Jimmy, and *CWA2:* 322–23, 324, 330–31; *CWB1:* 76

Chile and *CWA2:* 308; *CWB2:* 263

communism and *CWA2:* 263; *CWB2:* 250

Cuba and *CWA2:* 208, 215; *CWB1:* 84–85

Cultural Revolution and *CWA2:* 266–67, 293–95

Great Terror and *CWA1:* 120–23

Guatemala and *CWA1:* 180

Latin America and *CWA2:* 308, 324, 330–31, 339–40

Nicaragua and *CWA2:* 330–31

Reagan, Ronald, and *CWA2:* 339–40; *CWB2:* 395–97

Republic of China and *CWB1:* 98

United States of America and *CWB1:* 76, 84–85; *CWB2:* 250–51, 263

U.S. protests and *CWA2:* 268, 275–77, 279, 280–81

"Dictatorships and Double Standards" *CWB2:* 250

Dies Committee. *See* House Un-American Activities Committee (HUAC)

Dies, Martin *CWA1:* 101, 104–5; *CWPS:* 143 (ill.), 146–47

Diplomacy *CWB1:* 1; *CWB2:* 463, 467–70,

472; *CWPS:* 9, 14, 72, 75, 173

Disarmament. *See also* Military
Bush, George, and *CWPS:* 303–4, 305, 308, 311, 322, 323

Eisenhower, Dwight D., and *CWPS:* 102–3, 107–8, 109, 118

Gorbachev, Mikhail, and *CWPS:* 286, 287–96, 299–300, 302–4, 305–6, 308, 314

Khrushchev, Nikita, and *CWPS:* 195, 197, 201, 219

Reagan, Ronald, and *CWPS:* 286, 287–96, 303

Roosevelt, Eleanor, on *CWPS:* 94–95

Shultz, George, and *CWPS:* 303

Soviet Union and *CWPS:* 94–95, 286, 287–96, 299–300, 302–4, 305–6, 314

Yeltsin, Boris, and *CWPS:* 322, 323

Discrimination *CWB1:* 73, 198; *CWB2:* 402–3, 435. *See also* Racism; Segregation

Distinguished Flying Cross *CWB1:* 54

Dixiecrats *CWB2:* 460

DMZ. *See* Demilitarized Zone (DMZ)

DNC. *See* Democratic National Committee (DNC)

Dobrynin, Anatoly *CWA2:* 215, 226, 228–29; *CWPS:* 250–51, 253–55

Dockers' Union *CWB1:* 34

Dr. Strangelove CWA2: 236, 236 (ill.)

Doctor Zhivago CWB2: 234

Dole, Robert *CWB1:* 74

Dominican Republic *CWA2:* 264–65; *CWB1:* 203

Domino theory *CWB1:* 181, 198
Acheson, Dean G., and *CWPS:* 70, 222

China and *CWPS:* 70

communism and *CWPS:* 35–36, 40

Greece and *CWPS:* 35–36, 40

Khrushchev, Nikita, and *CWPS:* 221–22

Soviet Union and *CWPS:* 221–22

Turkey and *CWPS:* 35–36, 40

Vietnam War and *CWPS:* 41

Double agents. *See* Moles

Douglas, Helen Gahagan *CWB2:* 355

DPRK (Democratic People's Republic of Korea). *See* North Korea

Draft *CWA2:* 284–85, 336; *CWB1:* 76

DRV. *See* Democratic Republic of Vietnam (DRV)

Duarte, José Napoleón *CWA2:* 339

Dubcek, Alexander *CWA2:* 252, 253, 267–68; *CWB1:* 47; *CWB2:* 449

Dukakis, Michael *CWB1:* 56

Dulles, Allen *CWA1:* 119 (ill.), 154, 176; *CWA2:* 208; *CWB1:* 124

Dulles, Eleanor *CWB1:* 125

Dulles, John Foster *CWA1:* 175 (ill.), 180 (ill.); *CWB1:* 7, 124 (ill.), **124–33,** 129 (ill.); *CWB2:* 256, 307, 469; *CWPS:* 110, 119, 169 (ill.), 220
asymmetrical response and *CWA1:* 173–74

brinkmanship and *CWA1:* 167–69

nation building and *CWA1:* 179

nuclear weapons and *CWA1:* 171

Dumbarton Oaks Conference *CWA1:* 12; *CWB1:* 161

Dzerzhinski, Feliks *CWA1:* 160, 161 (ill.)

E

Early warning systems *CWB2:* 421

East Berlin *CWA1:* 72 (ill.), 73 (ill.), 75 (ill.), 76 (ill.); *CWB2:* 224, 235–36; *CWPS:* 205, 229. *See also* Berlin
as capital city *CWA1:* 68
détente and *CWA2:* 306
government of *CWA1:* 69–71; *CWA2:* 201
Soviet Union and *CWA1:* 69–71

East Germany *CWA1:* 60 (ill.). *See also* Germany
Brandt, Willy, and *CWB1:* 15
communism in *CWA1:* 30–31; *CWB2:* 268
Communist Party in *CWA2:* 358–59
democracy in *CWA2:* 358–59; *CWB2:* 421
economy of *CWA1:* 68–69, 71, 73; *CWA2:* 260; *CWB2:* 225, 272, 275; *CWPS:* 205–7, 223
Eisenhower, Dwight D., and *CWB1:* 130
elections in *CWA2:* 359, 363
formation of *CWA1:* 30–31, 38, 55, 68; *CWB1:* 12, 138; *CWB2:* 224, 235, 268, 432; *CWPS:* 204–5
Gorbachev, Mikhail, and *CWA2:* 358–59; *CWB1:* 58; *CWPS:* 230
government of *CWA1:* 68
independence of *CWA2:* 201

Khrushchev, Nikita, and *CWB2:* 224–25; *CWPS:* 207, 208, 210
Kohl, Helmut, and *CWB2:* 271–72
Marshall Plan and *CWB2:* 272
Nixon, Richard M., and *CWB1:* 14
Ostopolitik and *CWA2:* 305–6; *CWB1:* 15
refugees from *CWA1:* 68–69, 71, 73; *CWPS:* 205–7, 209, 210, 215, 221, 223, 224, 225
Soviet Union and *CWA1:* 68, 69–71; *CWA2:* 358–59; *CWB1:* 58, 129–30; *CWB2:* 224–25; *CWPS:* 207, 208, 209, 210, 230
West Germany and *CWB1:* 15; *CWB2:* 271–72

"Easter Parade" *CWA1:* 66

Eastern Bloc. *See also* Iron Curtain; "Iron Curtain speech"
Castro, Fidel, and *CWB1:* 86
collapse of *CWB2:* 421–22
communism in *CWB2:* 273–74; *CWPS:* 16–24, 295–96, 307, 309, 315
composition of *CWA1:* 105
"Crimes of Stalin" speech and *CWPS:* 182
Cuba and *CWB1:* 86
democracy in *CWA2:* 357–60; *CWPS:* 54, 56
economy of *CWB2:* 448; *CWPS:* 45
elections in *CWPS:* 18
formation of *CWPS:* 3, 17
Gorbachev, Mikhail, and *CWB2:* 421–22
Great Terror in *CWA1:* 121
Helsinki Accords and *CWB2:* 265
Khrushchev, Nikita, and *CWA2:* 193–96

Marshall Plan and *CWB2:* 325; *CWPS:* 30, 48, 57
peace and *CWPS:* 107, 108
reform in *CWA2:* 268
Shevardnadze, Eduard, and *CWB2:* 421–22
Soviet Union and *CWA2:* 193–96, 349; *CWB2:* 351, 446–48, 458; *CWPS:* 17–18, 30, 36, 45, 54, 56, 108
Stalin, Joseph, and *CWB2:* 425, 432, 446–48; *CWPS:* 17–18, 30, 36

ECA. *See* Economic Cooperation Administration (ECA)

Ecker, William *CWPS:* 258

Economic Cooperation Administration (ECA) *CWB2:* 325

Economy. *See also* Agriculture; Industry
Adenauer, Konrad, and *CWB1:* 9, 12, 14
African Americans and *CWA2:* 278, 281, 282
agriculture and *CWPS:* 46
Alliance for Progress and *CWA2:* 262–63
Andropov, Yuri, and *CWB2:* 417
of Asia *CWPS:* 271, 272
Attlee, Clement R., and *CWB1:* 28–29, 32
of Berlin *CWA1:* 55–56, 65–66, 68–69; *CWA2:* 200
Bevin, Ernest, and *CWB1:* 38
Bolshevik Revolution and *CWA1:* 6
Brezhnev, Leonid, and *CWB1:* 46, 51
Bush, George, and *CWA2:* 362; *CWPS:* 308, 309–11, 323, 324–25
capitalism and *CWA1:* 4, 27, 28, 56, 58, 104, 126, 168, 169–70; *CWA2:* 192, 214, 216, 298, 299,

320, 348, 372–73;
CWB1: 3, 26, 42, 86,
111, 119, 127, 150, 178;
CWB2: 211, 237,
251–52, 313, 385, 404;
CWPS: 1

Carter, Jimmy, and
CWB1: 76–77; *CWB2:*
391

Castro, Fidel, and *CWB1:*
86–87, 88, 91; *CWPS:*
232

of Chile *CWB1:* 21–23;
CWB2: 263, 362

of China *CWA1:* 52;
CWA2: 206; *CWB1:* 96,
116, 118–19, 121–23;
CWB2: 313, 317–18,
470–71

Clinton, Bill, and *CWPS:*
324

Cold War and *CWA1:*
24–25

Colombo Plan and
CWB1: 40

Common Market and
CWB1: 14

Commonwealth of Inde-
pendent States (CIS)
and *CWA2:* 370

communism and *CWA1:*
2, 3, 27–29, 56, 57, 80,
99, 100, 126, 128, 167,
168, 169–70; *CWA2:*
192, 214, 215, 234, 251,
252, 262, 276, 290–92,
298, 299, 319–20, 348,
352; *CWB1:* 3, 18, 26,
42, 82, 100, 110, 127,
150, 160, 168, 178, 186;
CWB2: 211, 223, 231,
250, 251, 278, 295, 312,
331, 340, 346, 366, 385,
389, 404, 410, 426, 445,
458, 464; *CWPS:* 1–2, 4,
204

containment and *CWA1:*
28, 31–32, 35–36,
49–50, 51; *CWPS:* 9, 44,
52–59, 61, 75

of Cuba *CWA2:* 208,
209–10, 215, 216–17;

CWB1: 84–85, 86–87,
88, 91; *CWPS:* 232

of Czechoslovakia *CWA2:*
267

democracy and *CWA2:*
262; *CWB2:* 426

Deng Xiaoping and
CWB1: 116, 118–19,
121–23

of East Germany *CWA1:*
68–69, 71, 73; *CWA2:*
260; *CWB2:* 225, 272,
275

of East Berlin *CWPS:* 229

of East Germany *CWPS:*
205–7, 223

of Eastern Bloc *CWB2:*
448; *CWPS:* 45

of Europe *CWB1:* 14,
30–31, 38; *CWB2:*
308–9, 324–26; *CWPS:*
9, 27, 30, 43–50, 61

of France *CWB1:* 12;
CWPS: 33, 58

freedom and *CWPS:* 47

of Germany *CWA1:* 57,
58–59; *CWA2:* 372

global *CWA1:* 12, 13,
23–24, 25, 32

Gorbachev, Mikhail, and
CWA2: 362; *CWB1:* 56,
154–55, 157; *CWB2:*
395, 414, 418, 442;
CWPS: 283–85, 296,
299, 300, 301, 302, 308,
313, 315

of Great Britain *CWA1:*
17; *CWB1:* 28–29, 32,
38, 39, 170; *CWB2:*
305–6, 308–9, 310,
439–40; *CWPS:* 58

Great Depression and
CWA1: 103–4

Great Leap Forward and
CWB2: 317–18

of Greece *CWPS:* 34, 37,
39–40, 58

Harriman, W. Averell, and
CWB1: 172

of Iceland *CWPS:* 58

of Italy *CWPS:* 33, 58

of Japan *CWA1:* 42;
CWA2: 372; *CWB2:*
297, 298, 299

Khrushchev, Nikita, and
CWA2: 292; *CWB2:*
239; *CWPS:* 120,
189–90

Kim Il Sung and *CWB2:*
244–45, 247

Kohl, Helmut, and
CWB2: 272

Kosygin, Aleksey, and
CWB2: 277, 279,
280–81

Macmillan, Harold, and
CWB2: 305–6, 310

Mao Zedong and *CWB1:*
118–19

Marshall, George C., and
CWB2: 321, 324–26

Marshall Plan and *CWA1:*
28, 31–32; *CWB1:* 4,
30–31, 38, 113; *CWPS:*
33, 43–50, 52, 54,
56–59, 61

Marxism and *CWA1:* 6

military and *CWA1:*
173–74; *CWA2:* 275,
277–78, 290; *CWPS:*
119–20, 265

military-industrial com-
plexes and *CWA2:* 275,
277–78, 290

Molotov Plan and *CWA1:*
28, 32–34; *CWPS:* 45

nationalization of *CWB1:*
21, 22, 23, 28–29, 86;
CWB2: 263, 362,
380–81

of Nicaragua *CWA2:* 332

Nixon, Richard M., and
CWPS: 271, 272

of North Korea *CWB2:*
244–45, 247

nuclear weapons and
CWPS: 119–20

Reagan, Ronald, and
CWB2: 392; *CWPS:*
265

Roosevelt, Franklin D.,
and *CWA1:* 5, 12–13,
103–4; *CWB1:* 64;
CWB2: 295, 389

of Russia *CWA2:* 373; *CWB1:* 58–59; *CWB2:* 346, 380; *CWPS:* 323, 324

Shevardnadze, Eduard, and *CWB2:* 418

socialism and *CWB1:* 86

of Soviet Union *CWA1:* 17, 174–75; *CWA2:* 277, 278, 290–92, 303, 304, 337, 338, 343, 347–52, 361, 362, 367–68; *CWB1:* 3, 46, 51, 56, 146, 154–55, 157; *CWB2:* 239, 277, 279, 280–81, 361, 395, 396, 414, 417, 418, 429, 442, 448; *CWPS:* 23, 27–28, 99, 120, 189–90, 209, 265, 283–85, 296, 299, 300, 302, 308, 309–11, 313, 315

Stalin, Joseph, and *CWB2:* 429

of Taiwan *CWB1:* 98

Thatcher, Margaret, and *CWB2:* 439–40

Third World and *CWA2:* 252, 254, 307

Tito, Josip Broz, and *CWB2:* 448, 451

Truman, Harry S., and *CWB2:* 459

of Turkey *CWPS:* 34, 38, 39–40

of United States of America *CWA1:* 17; *CWA2:* 304, 338–39, 362, 372–73; *CWB1:* 3, 4, 26, 60, 64, 71, 76–77, 84–85, 86–87, 204; *CWB2:* 294–95, 323, 369–70, 389, 391, 392, 455, 459

Vietnam War and *CWB1:* 204

of West Berlin *CWPS:* 229

of West Germany *CWA1:* 62–66, 67–68, 68–69; *CWB1:* 9, 12, 14; *CWB2:* 272; *CWPS:* 205–7

Yeltsin, Boris, and *CWA2:* 373; *CWB1:* 58–59; *CWPS:* 296, 323, 324

Yugoslavia and *CWA1:* 51; *CWB2:* 448, 451

EDC. *See* European Defense Community (EDC)

Edemski, Sergei A. *CWA1:* 153

Eden, Anthony *CWB2:* 305, 306, 306 (ill.)

Education. *See also* School communism and *CWPS:* 127–32, 141–42, 146, 148–65, 174

of Khrushchev, Nikita *CWPS:* 174, 175

EEC. *See* European Economic Community (EEC)

Egypt *CWA2:* 202–3, 204–5, 309–10, 328–30

Brezhnev, Leonid, and *CWB1:* 50

Camp David Accords and *CWB2:* 263

independence of *CWB1:* 29

October War and *CWB1:* 50; *CWB2:* 262–63

Six-Day War and *CWB1:* 203

Soviet Union and *CWB1:* 50; *CWB2:* 262–63

Suez War and *CWB1:* 131–32, 142; *CWB2:* 306

Einstein, Albert *CWA1:* 81, 94; *CWA2:* 244; *CWB2:* 369

Eisenhower Doctrine *CWA2:* 192, 203–5; *CWB1:* 132, 142

Eisenhower, Dwight D. *CWA1:* 119 (ill.), 188 (ill.); *CWB1:* 129 (ill.), 134 (ill.), **134–45**, 137 (ill.), 138 (ill.); *CWPS:* 101 (ill.), 104 (ill.), 109 (ill.), 114 (ill.), 117 (ill.), 120 (ill.)

Acheson, Dean G., and *CWB1:* 6, 7

"Atoms for Peace" plan of *CWB1:* 140–41

as author *CWB1:* 139, 144; *CWPS:* 100

Bay of Pigs and *CWB1:* 144; *CWPS:* 233

Berlin and *CWB1:* 137; *CWPS:* 209

brinkmanship and *CWA2:* 203–4; *CWPS:* 119–20

budget and *CWPS:* 102, 119–20

Camp David and *CWA2:* 201

Castro, Fidel, and *CWB1:* 87; *CWB2:* 223; *CWPS:* 233

"The Chance for Peace" speech of *CWPS:* 89, **99–112,** 188

character of *CWB1:* 143

China and *CWA1:* 184; *CWB1:* 130

Cold War and *CWA1:* 52

communism and *CWB1:* 140–41, 181

containment and *CWA2:* 202; *CWB1:* 141, 142

Cuba and *CWA2:* 208–10, 216–17, 258; *CWB1:* 87, 143–44; *CWB2:* 223; *CWPS:* 233

death of *CWB1:* 144–45

disarmament and *CWPS:* 102–3, 107–8, 109, 118

Dulles, John Foster, and *CWB1:* 128–30, 131

early life of *CWB1:* 134–35

East Germany and *CWB1:* 130

Egypt and *CWA2:* 203

Eisenhower Doctrine and *CWA2:* 203–4; *CWB1:* 142

election of *CWA1:* 48, 118, 170; *CWB1:* 128, 139–40, 141–42, 143; *CWB2:* 302, 334, 356, 389, 461; *CWPS:* 99–100, 100–101, 110, 184–85, 187 espionage and *CWA1:* 152; *CWA2:* 198, 240; *CWB1:* 144; *CWB2:* 308; *CWPS:* 202

France and *CWA1:* 181

Germany and *CWB1:* 138; *CWPS:* 100, 209

Guatemala and *CWB1:* 141

Hungary and *CWB1:* 130, 142

imperialism and *CWB1:* 87, 141, 144; *CWB2:* 223

Iran and *CWB1:* 141

Jordan and *CWA2:* 204

Kennan, George F., and *CWB2:* 215

Khrushchev, Nikita, and *CWA1:* 185–88; *CWA2:* 193, 200–201, 205, 210–12, 240; *CWB1:* 141, 144; *CWB2:* 230, 237, 238, 308; *CWPS:* 188–89, 191–92, 195, 197, 200–201, 202, 209

Korean War and *CWA1:* 48; *CWB1:* 134, 140, 143; *CWPS:* 106–7, 108

Lebanon and *CWA2:* 204

loyalty programs and *CWA1:* 171

MacArthur, Douglas, and *CWB1:* 135

Macmillan, Harold, and *CWB2:* 305, 307, 308

Malenkov, Georgy M., and *CWA1:* 170–71

McCarthy, Joseph R., and *CWA1:* 118; *CWB1:* 140; *CWB2:* 334; *CWPS:* 111, 171–72

military and *CWB1:* 134, 135–39; *CWPS:* 119–20, 191, 202

missiles and *CWA2:* 198–99; *CWB2:* 307

Mosaddeq, Mohammed, and *CWA1:* 178

nation building and *CWA1:* 177, 178–80

Nixon, Richard M., and *CWB1:* 139–40; *CWB2:*

356, 358; *CWPS:* 100–101

North Atlantic Treaty Organization and *CWB1:* 139; *CWPS:* 100, 105–6

nuclear energy and *CWA2:* 241

nuclear war and *CWPS:* 116–17, 192

nuclear weapons and *CWA1:* 70, 170–71; *CWA2:* 200–201; *CWB1:* 140, 144; *CWB2:* 215; *CWPS:* 89, 102, 113–21

"Open Skies" plan of *CWA1:* 186–87; *CWB1:* 140–41; *CWPS:* 102–3, 188–89

Oppenheimer, J. Robert, and *CWB2:* 376

peace and *CWB1:* 134; *CWPS:* 88–89, 99–111, 113–21, 188, 192

"Peaceful Uses of Atomic Energy" speech of *CWPS:* 89, 113–21

popularity of *CWB1:* 143

presidency of *CWB1:* 139–44

Reagan, Ronald, and *CWB2:* 389

reconnaissance and *CWA1:* 148, 150; *CWA2:* 211–12

religion and *CWPS:* 111

Republic of China and *CWB1:* 141

retirement of *CWB1:* 144

Roosevelt, Franklin D., and *CWB1:* 136; *CWPS:* 100

Southeast Asia Treaty Organization and *CWB1:* 141

Soviet Union and *CWB1:* 137, 138, 140–41, 142, 143; *CWPS:* 102, 110, 187

space race and *CWB1:* 142

Stalin, Joseph, and *CWB1:* 138; *CWPS:* 100

Suez War and *CWA2:* 203; *CWB1:* 131–32, 142; *CWB2:* 306

Taiwan and *CWA1:* 184; *CWB1:* 130

television and *CWB1:* 143

Third World and *CWB1:* 141

Truman, Harry S., and *CWB1:* 139; *CWPS:* 100

United Nations and *CWPS:* 113–19

U.S. Congress and *CWPS:* 81

Vietnam and *CWA1:* 181–82; *CWA2:* 283; *CWB1:* 141

Vietnam War and *CWB1:* 198

West Berlin and *CWA1:* 70; *CWB1:* 132; *CWB2:* 237

World War I and *CWB1:* 135

World War II and *CWB1:* 134, 135–38; *CWPS:* 99–100, 103

on World War III *CWPS:* 105

Eisler, Gerhart *CWPS:* 161

El Salvador *CWA2:* 331, 339

ELAS. *See* National Popular Liberation Army (ELAS)

Elections
of 1932 *CWB1:* 2, 64, 170
of 1944 *CWB2:* 456
of 1948 *CWA1:* 107; *CWB1:* 139; *CWB2:* 389, 459, 460
of 1952 *CWA1:* 48, 117, 118; *CWB1:* 128, 139–40, 143 (ill.); *CWB2:* 301–2, 334, 356, 389, 461; *CWPS:* 99–100, 100–101, 110, 184–85, 187
of 1956 *CWB1:* 141–42, 143
of 1958 *CWB2:* 389

of 1960 *CWA1:* 70; *CWA2:* 212, 251; *CWB1:* 113, 197; *CWB2:* 221, 358, 390; *CWPS:* 191, 209

of 1964 *CWA2:* 270; *CWB1:* 199–200; *CWB2:* 358, 390

of 1968 *CWA2:* 273, 312; *CWB1:* 204; *CWB2:* 257, 358, 390

of 1972 *CWA2:* 312; *CWB2:* 259, 362, 390; *CWPS:* 264

of 1976 *CWA2:* 314–15; *CWB1:* 55, 74; *CWB2:* 390; *CWPS:* 265

of 1980 *CWA2:* 335, 337–38; *CWB1:* 55–56, 79; *CWB2:* 251; *CWPS:* 142, 265, 284

of 1984 *CWA2:* 344–45; *CWB1:* 56; *CWB2:* 395; *CWPS:* 265, 283

of 1988 *CWB1:* 56; *CWB2:* 399; *CWPS:* 294–95

of 1992 *CWB1:* 60; *CWPS:* 324–25

of 1996 *CWA2:* 373

of 2000 *CWA2:* 373; *CWB1:* 61; *CWB2:* 406

Carter, Jimmy, monitors *CWB1:* 80–81

Castro, Fidel, and *CWPS:* 232

in Chile *CWB1:* 19, 20–21

communism and *CWA1:* 2, 3, 27, 28, 56, 57, 80, 99, 100, 105, 126, 128, 168; *CWA2:* 192, 214, 215, 234, 251, 252, 276, 298, 320, 348; *CWB1:* 162; *CWB2:* 295; *CWPS:* 1, 149, 151, 156, 160, 204

Communist Party and *CWA1:* 27

in Cuba *CWA2:* 216; *CWPS:* 232

in Czechoslovakia *CWA2:* 360

democracy and *CWA1:* 4, 27, 58, 128, 167–68; *CWA2:* 192, 214, 216, 276, 298, 299, 320; *CWB1:* 25–26, 42, 86, 127; *CWB2:* 251, 271, 314, 385, 404, 426, 449; *CWPS:* 1

in East Germany *CWA1:* 68; *CWA2:* 359, 363

in Eastern Bloc *CWPS:* 18

in France *CWB1:* 14

in Germany *CWB2:* 274

Gorbachev, Mikhail, and *CWPS:* 304–5

in Great Britain *CWA1:* 15; *CWB1:* 27, 28, 33, 40, 106, 107; *CWB2:* 304, 305, 306, 308, 437; *CWPS:* 16

in Hungary *CWA2:* 358

in Italy *CWPS:* 49

in North Korea *CWB2:* 247

in Poland *CWA2:* 357–58; *CWB1:* 36–37, 66, 171; *CWB2:* 431

Red Scare and *CWA1:* 106

in Russia *CWA2:* 373

in Soviet Union *CWA1:* 52; *CWA2:* 255–56, 360–61; *CWB1:* 41, 44, 45, 152–53, 157, 163, 166; *CWB2:* 210–11, 232; *CWPS:* 99, 187–88, 265, 283, 304–5

Stalin, Joseph, and *CWB1:* 138

in Supreme Soviet *CWPS:* 5

in United States of America *CWB1:* 25–26

in Vietnam *CWA1:* 182

in West Germany *CWA1:* 67, 173; *CWB1:* 12, 15; *CWB2:* 271

Yalta agreements and *CWA1:* 105

Yalta Conference and *CWPS:* 18

in Yugoslavia *CWB2:* 450

Elizabeth II *CWB1:* 100–101

Ellis, Frank *CWPS:* 212

Elsey, George *CWA1:* 22; *CWB1:* 111

Emergency Powers Act *CWB1:* 35

Empire Ken CWA2: 203 (ill.)

"End of Cold War: Address Before a Joint Session of the Congress on the State of the Union, January 28, 1992" *CWPS:* 319–26

Energy *CWB1:* 76–77. *See also* Nuclear energy

Enola Gay CWA1: 87–88

"Enormous" *CWA1:* 90–91

Enrico Fermi Award *CWB2:* 377

Espionage *CWA1:* 136, 137 (ill.), 146 (ill.), 149 (ill.). *See also* Intelligence; Moles; Reconnaissance
Ames, Aldrich, and *CWA1:* 162

Berlin tunnel and *CWA1:* 145–46, 146 (ill.)

Boyce, Christopher, and *CWA1:* 154–55

Cambridge Spies and *CWA1:* 135, 140–44

Central Intelligence Agency (CIA) and *CWA1:* 34, 143, 145–46, 154, 158, 162

China and *CWA1:* 158–59

Churchill, Winston, and *CWA1:* 140, 142

Cold War and *CWA1:* 24, 127–29, 129–32

communism and *CWPS:* 170

definition of *CWA1:* 125–26

Eisenhower, Dwight D., and *CWA1:* 152; *CWA2:* 198, 240; *CWB1:* 144; *CWB2:* 308; *CWPS:* 202

execution and *CWA1:* 140, 152, 158, 162

Federal Bureau of Investigation (FBI) and *CWA1:* 131, 143, 163

Gorbachev, Mikhail, and *CWA1:* 157

Gordievsky, Oleg, and *CWA1:* 157

Great Britain and *CWA1:* 127, 131, 136–38, 140–44, 145–46, 151–52, 157

GRU (Soviet military intelligence agency) and *CWA1:* 154

Hanssen, Robert Philip, and *CWA1:* 162–63

Hiss, Alger, and *CWA1:* 44, 135

history of *CWA1:* 126–27

House Un-American Activities Committee and *CWPS:* 147–48

human element of *CWA1:* 150–51

Israel and *CWA1:* 159–60

Johnson, Lyndon B., and *CWB1:* 203

Jordan and *CWA1:* 161

Kennedy, John F., and *CWA1:* 152

KGB (Soviet secret police) and *CWA1:* 140, 141–42, 144

Khrushchev, Nikita, and *CWA2:* 240; *CWB1:* 144; *CWB2:* 238, 308; *CWPS:* 202

Korean War and *CWA1:* 143

Lee, Andrew Daulton, and *CWA1:* 154–55

listening stations and *CWA1:* 144–45

Manhattan Project and *CWA1:* 88–89, 90–91, 115, 128, 138, 139; *CWB1:* 191–92; *CWB2:* 285, 287, 351; *CWPS:* 5, 73, 133

Marshall Plan and *CWPS:* 50

media and *CWA1:* 143

military and *CWA1:* 131

Military Intelligence, Department 5 and *CWA1:* 142

Military Intelligence, Department 6 and *CWA1:* 142, 143, 145–46, 152

National Security Agency (NSA) and *CWA1:* 131

North Korea and *CWB1:* 203

nuclear weapons and *CWA1:* 9, 14, 19, 43, 88–89, 90–91, 108, 115, 128, 135–40, 143; *CWA2:* 197–98; *CWB1:* 191–92; *CWB2:* 285, 287, 333, 351; *CWPS:* 5, 73, 133

Philby, Kim, and *CWA1:* 140–41, 142, 143, 144

photography and *CWA1:* 137 (ill.), 147–50; *CWA2:* 198, 222

Pollard, Jonathan Jay, and *CWA1:* 159–60

radio and *CWA1:* 143

Reagan, Ronald, and *CWA1:* 157

reconnaissance and *CWA1:* 147–50

Red Scare and *CWA1:* 44, 107, 112, 113–14

Roosevelt, Franklin D., and *CWA1:* 140, 142

satellites and *CWA1:* 150, 154–55

Sombolay, Albert, and *CWA1:* 161

Soviet Union and *CWA1:* 9, 14, 19, 43, 60, 88–89, 90–91, 127, 132, 136–45, 146, 148–50, 151, 152, 153, 154–58, 160, 162, 163–64; *CWPS:* 5, 73, 133

space race and *CWB1:* 142

Stalin, Joseph, and *CWA1:* 140, 142–43

tradecraft of *CWA1:* 136–37, 141

Truman, Harry S., and *CWA1:* 140, 142

types of *CWA1:* 141

U-2 aircraft and *CWA1:* 127, 147–50; *CWA2:* 211, 240, 310

U.S. Army and *CWA1:* 145–46, 153, 161

U.S. Navy and *CWA1:* 155–57

VENONA *CWA1:* 127, 132–35, 133 (ill.), 138, 140, 143

Walker spy ring and *CWA1:* 155–57

Watergate scandal and *CWB2:* 363, 364

West Germany and *CWA1:* 60

World War I and *CWA1:* 126–27, 149

World War II and *CWA1:* 127, 131, 140, 142–43, 149; *CWA2:* 224

Wu-Tai Chin, Larry, and *CWA1:* 158–59

Yurchenko, Vitaly, and *CWA1:* 158

Estonia *CWA2:* 361–62, 369

Ethiopia *CWA2:* 325–26, 326 (ill.); *CWB1:* 50, 164

Ethnic conflict *CWA2:* 315, 324, 374–76. *See also* Racism

Europe *CWA1:* 106 (ill.); *CWA2:* 371 (ill.). *See also* specific countries and regions

Brezhnev, Leonid, on *CWB1:* 41

capitalism and *CWPS:* 2–3

Charter of Paris and *CWPS:* 317

communism and *CWPS:* 56

democracy and *CWPS:* 2–3

détente and *CWA2:* 299, 305–6, 337

economy of *CWB1:* 14, 30–31, 38; *CWB2:* 308–9, 324–26; *CWPS:* 9, 27, 30, 43–50, 61

Marshall Plan and *CWB2:* 324–25; *CWPS:* 9, 30, 43–50, 52–59, 61
military and *CWB2:* 262
peace and *CWA2:* 364–67
unification of *CWB2:* 269–70, 272, 273
World War II and *CWPS:* 27

European Advisory Commission *CWB2:* 210

European Common Market. *See* Common Market

European Defense Community (EDC) *CWB1:* 12; *CWPS:* 106

European Economic Community (EEC). *See* Common Market

European Recovery Program for Western Europe. *See* Marshall Plan

Ex-Comm *CWA2:* 221–25; *CWPS:* 234, 236–37, 238–43

Execution *CWPS:* 179. *See also* Death
Cuban Revolution and *CWA2:* 208
Cultural Revolution and *CWA2:* 266–67, 294
espionage and *CWA1:* 140, 152, 158, 162
Great Terror and *CWA1:* 120, 121, 188; *CWA2:* 192
KGB (Soviet secret police) and *CWA1:* 127, 132

Executive Order 9835 *CWA1:* 107

F

Fabian Society *CWB1:* 26
Facism *CWB1:* 185–86, 189–90
Fair Deal *CWB2:* 459
Fanfani, Amintore *CWPS:* 220
FAPSI. *See* Federal Agency for Government Communications and Information (FAPSI)

Far East *CWA1:* 182; *CWA2:* 265. *See also* specific countries

Farouk (king of Egypt) *CWA2:* 202

Farrell, Thomas *CWA1:* 79–80; *CWB2:* 372

Fascism *CWPS:* 158

Fat Man *CWA1:* 85, 87–88, 90, 91

FBI. *See* Federal Bureau of Investigation (FBI)

Fear *CWPS:* 123, 185, 186, 198
Cold War and *CWA1:* 105, 128–29
of communism *CWA1:* 99–100; *CWA2:* 372
McCarthyism and *CWA1:* 101, 116, 118
of nuclear war *CWA2:* 372, 374
Red Scare and *CWA1:* 11, 105

February Revolution *CWB2:* 347. *See also* Bolshevik Revolution

Fechter, Peter *CWA1:* 74

Federal Agency for Government Communications and Information (FAPSI) *CWA1:* 160

Federal Bureau of Investigation (FBI) *CWA1:* 130 (ill.); *CWPS:* 125–32, 130 (ill.), 133, 161. *See also* Hoover, J. Edgar; Intelligence
civil rights and *CWB1:* 187, 193
communism and *CWB1:* 186, 189–92
corruption and *CWB1:* 188
definition of *CWA1:* 126
democracy and *CWB1:* 186, 189–90
espionage and *CWA1:* 131, 143, 163
facism and *CWB1:* 189–90

formation of *CWA1:* 131
freedom and *CWA1:* 108–9
Great Depression and *CWB1:* 188–89
Hoover, J. Edgar, becomes director of *CWB1:* 187–88
Manhattan Project and *CWB1:* 191–92
organized crime and *CWB1:* 189
Prohibition Era and *CWB1:* 185
propaganda and *CWA1:* 108
Red Scare and *CWA1:* 100, 107, 108; *CWB1:* 189–92
science and *CWB1:* 188
Watergate scandal and *CWB2:* 363
World War II and *CWB1:* 189–90

Federal Council of Churches of Christ in America *CWB1:* 126

Federal Republic of Germany. *See* West Germany

Federalism *CWB2:* 450

Felix, Antonia *CWB2:* 403, 404, 407

Fellow travelers *CWPS:* 157, 158

"Feminine factor" *CWB2:* 439

Ferguson, Francis *CWB2:* 368

Fermi, Enrico *CWB2:* 284, 371, 375, 377

Fifth Amendment *CWA1:* 110, 113; *CWPS:* 142

Filatov, Anatoli Nikolaevich *CWA1:* 154

First Lightning *CWA1:* 90

Fission *CWA1:* 80, 81, 87; *CWB2:* 284–85, 409

Ford Motor Company *CWB2:* 339, 342

Ford, Gerald R. *CWA2:* 310–11, 314, 315; *CWB1:* 49 (ill.); *CWPS:* 265
Brezhnev, Leonid, and *CWB1:* 48–49

Bush, George, and *CWB1:* 55

détente and *CWB1:* 49

election of 1976 and *CWB1:* 74

Kissinger, Henry, and *CWB2:* 264–65

Nixon, Richard M., and *CWB1:* 74; *CWB2:* 364

nuclear weapons and *CWB1:* 166

Reagan, Ronald, and *CWB2:* 266, 390

Rockefeller, Nelson A., and *CWB1:* 55

Strategic Arms Limitation Talks and *CWB1:* 166

Foreign Intelligence Advisory Board *CWB1:* 113

Foreign Service *CWB2:* 208

Forester's Cabin *CWA1:* 90

Forrestal, James V. *CWA1:* 22

Foster, William Z. *CWPS:* 148, 150, 153, 160

The Fountainhead CWB2: 383; *CWPS:* 136

Four Modernizations *CWB2:* 320

Four Point Program *CWA1:* 49–50

Four-power Allied Control Council *CWA1:* 15

Four-Power Summit Conference *CWPS:* 188

France *CWPS:* 33, 43, 49, 58

Adenauer, Konrad, and *CWB1:* 12, 14

Berlin airlift and *CWA1:* 63

colonialism and *CWA2:* 206, 268–69; *CWB1:* 177–78, 180

Communist Party in *CWA1:* 31; *CWB1:* 178

détente and *CWA2:* 306

economy of *CWB1:* 12

Egypt and *CWA2:* 203

elections in *CWB1:* 14

Germany and *CWA1:* 59

Great Britain and *CWB2:* 308

Ho Chi Minh and *CWB1:* 177–78, 180; *CWB2:* 257

Indochina and *CWA1:* 42, 50, 181–82; *CWB1:* 177–78, 180

North Atlantic Treaty Organization (NATO) and *CWA2:* 203, 306

nuclear weapons and *CWA2:* 247, 373

Suez War and *CWA2:* 203; *CWB1:* 131–32, 142; *CWB2:* 306

Vietminh and *CWB1:* 180

Vietnam and *CWA1:* 42, 181–82; *CWA2:* 283; *CWB1:* 141, 177–78, 179, 180, 198; *CWB2:* 257, 469

West Germany and *CWB1:* 12, 13, 14

Western European Union (WEU) and *CWA1:* 37

World War II and *CWA1:* 3; *CWA2:* 364

Franco, Francisco *CWB1:* 84

Franco-German Friendship Treaty *CWB1:* 14

Frankfurter, Felix *CWB1:* 2

Franklin Delano Roosevelt Freedom from Want Medal *CWB2:* 343

FRAP. *See* Popular Revolutionary Action Front (FRAP)

Freedom. *See also* Civil rights; Human rights; specific freedoms

African Americans and *CWA2:* 275–76

Brezhnev, Leonid, and *CWB1:* 46, 47

Bush, George, and *CWPS:* 315, 320, 323

Cold War and *CWA2:* 347

communism and *CWA1:* 5, 20–21, 77, 99, 100–101; *CWA2:* 292; *CWB2:* 250, 381; *CWPS:* 36, 38–40, 72, 74, 151–52

Communist Party and *CWB2:* 434; *CWPS:* 299

in Czechoslovakia *CWB1:* 47

democracy and *CWA1:* 5, 27, 100–101, 103, 104–5, 107–12, 128; *CWA2:* 275–77; *CWPS:* 1, 36, 127, 228

economy and *CWPS:* 47

Federal Bureau of Investigation (FBI) and *CWA1:* 108–9

Germany and *CWPS:* 228–29

Gorbachev, Mikhail, and *CWPS:* 283, 290, 296, 299, 308, 314–15

Helsinki Accords and *CWB2:* 264–65

Ho Chi Minh and *CWB1:* 181–82

Kennedy, John F., and *CWPS:* 228–29

KGB (Soviet secret police) and *CWB1:* 46

Khrushchev, Nikita, and *CWB2:* 233, 234

Mao Zedong and *CWB2:* 312, 314, 318, 320

McNamara, Robert S., and *CWB2:* 337

Nixon, Richard M., and *CWPS:* 279

peace and *CWPS:* 54–55, 57

in Poland *CWA2:* 193–94

racism and *CWA2:* 275–76, 282–83

Reagan, Ronald, on *CWB2:* 387; *CWPS:* 284–85, 289

Red Scare and *CWA1:* 103, 104–5, 107–12; *CWB2:* 384

Sakharov, Andrey, and *CWB2:* 408, 412

Shevardnadze, Eduard, on *CWB2:* 416

in Soviet Union *CWA2:* 292, 348, 351, 357, 367;

CWB2: 233, 234, 408;
CWPS: 283, 296, 299
Stalin, Joseph, and CWA1:
100, 120; CWPS: 2
strength and CWPS: 278
Thatcher, Margaret, and
CWB2: 437, 442–43
Tito, Josip Broz, and
CWB2: 451
in Vietnam CWB1:
181–82
in Yugoslavia CWB2: 451
Freedom March CWB2: 222
Freedom of assembly
CWA1: 109, 110;
CWB1: 193
Freedom of religion CWA1:
128; CWB2: 385, 389;
CWPS: 2, 132, 138, 151,
152. See also Religion
communism and CWA1:
2, 3, 28, 56, 80, 99, 100,
126, 128, 167, 168;
CWA2: 192, 214, 234,
252, 276, 292, 298, 320,
348
democracy and CWA1: 4,
101, 128; CWA2: 192
in Soviet Union CWA2:
357
Freedom of speech CWB1:
193
communism and CWA2:
292
democracy and CWA1:
128; CWA2: 275–77
glasnost and CWA2: 351
Hollywood Ten and
CWA1: 110
Hoover, J. Edgar, and
CWA1: 109
Freedom of the press CWA2:
252, 267–68, 292
Frei Montalvá, Eduardo
CWA2: 264
Friedrichstrasse Crossing. See
Checkpoint Charlie
Fuchs, Klaus CWA1: 90–91,
128, 137–38; CWB1:
192; CWB2: 287
Fusion CWA1: 88; CWB2:
409

G

Gamsakhurdia, Zviad
CWB2: 422
Gang of Four CWB1: 119,
120; CWB2: 320
Gardner, Meredith CWA1:
134–35
Garst, Roswell CWPS: 197,
199
Garthoff, Raymond L.
CWA1: 125
The Gathering Storm CWPS:
16
GDR (German Democratic
Republic). See East Ger-
many
General Electric CWB2: 389
General Intelligence Divi-
sion CWA1: 103;
CWB1: 187. See also
Federal Bureau of Inves-
tigation (FBI)
Generation gap CWA2: 287
Geneva Conference CWB2:
469
George Bush Presidential Li-
brary CWB1: 61
Georgia (USSR) CWA2: 362;
CWB2: 417, 422–23
German Democratic Repub-
lic (GDR). See East Ger-
many
Germany CWA1: 59 (ill.), 60
(ill.), 61 (ill.). See also
East Germany; West
Germany
Bush, George, and CWA2:
363–64; CWB2: 405;
CWPS: 317
Byrnes, James F., and
CWB1: 67
capitalism and CWA1:
58–59
Christian Democratic
Union in CWB2: 274
Cold War and CWA1:
60–61
containment and CWA1:
58; CWB2: 432
Czechoslovakia and
CWA1: 34

democracy and CWA1:
58–59
division of CWA1: 30–31,
38, 66–69, 172–73;
CWB1: 12, 66, 105,
106–7, 138, 161;
CWB2: 224, 235, 268,
351–52, 432; CWPS:
204–5, 208, 217–18
economy of CWA1: 57,
58–59; CWA2: 372
Eisenhower, Dwight D.,
and CWB1: 138;
CWPS: 100, 209
elections in CWB2: 274
France and CWA1: 59
freedom and CWPS:
228–29
Gorbachev, Mikhail, and
CWA2: 363–64; CWB1:
58; CWB2: 405; CWPS:
317
government of CWA1: 15,
30–31, 55, 57–59;
CWB1: 138
Great Britain and CWA1:
58–59
Harriman, W. Averell, and
CWB1: 172
Kennan, George F., and
CWB2: 210
Kennedy, John F., and
CWPS: 210
Khrushchev, Nikita, and
CWPS: 221
Marshall, George C., and
CWPS: 40–41
Marshall Plan and CWPS:
48, 50
Molotov, Vyacheslav, and
CWB2: 348–50, 351
money in CWA1: 62
Nazi-Soviet Non-Aggres-
sion Pact and CWA1:
6–8
North Atlantic Treaty Or-
ganization (NATO) and
CWA2: 363–64; CWB1:
58; CWB2: 274
nuclear energy and
CWB2: 284–85
nuclear war and CWPS:
220

nuclear weapons and *CWA1:* 81–82, 85; *CWA2:* 200–201, 364; *CWB2:* 370, 371

Poland and *CWB2:* 431

reparations and *CWA1:* 15–17, 57, 58; *CWB1:* 66

reunification of *CWA1:* 172–73, 185–86; *CWA2:* 201, 363–64; *CWB1:* 12, 13–14, 53, 58; *CWB2:* 268, 272, 273–74, 351, 401, 405; *CWPS:* 106, 107, 205, 208, 217–18, 228–29, 317

Rice, Condoleezza, and *CWB2:* 401

Soviet Union and *CWA1:* 6–8, 29, 57; *CWA2:* 363–64; *CWB1:* 58, 106–7, 172; *CWB2:* 348, 351, 431, 432; *CWPS:* 20, 48, 205, 208, 217–18, 221, 317

Stalin, Joseph, and *CWB2:* 432

transportation and *CWA1:* 68–69

treaties concerning *CWB1:* 37; *CWB2:* 274

Truman, Harry S., and *CWB1:* 107

World War II and *CWA1:* 2, 3, 7–8, 8–9, 10, 11, 15–17, 29, 55, 56–57, 58–59; *CWA2:* 364; *CWB1:* 102–5, 106–7, 136–37, 161; *CWB2:* 348, 431; *CWPS:* 100

Ghana *CWA2:* 255

GID. *See* General Intelligence Division (GID)

Ginzburg, Vitali *CWA1:* 95

Glasnost *CWA2:* 348, 351, 367

Gorbachev, Mikhail, and *CWB1:* 56, 146, 153; *CWB2:* 274, 395, 414, 416, 418

Shevardnadze, Eduard, and *CWB2:* 416

Glassboro Summit *CWB2:* 281

Glenn, John H., Jr. *CWA2:* 198

G-Men *CWB1:* 188–89

Goebbels, Joseph *CWB2:* 273

Gold, Harry *CWA1:* 91, 108, 138; *CWPS:* 133

Goldwater, Barry *CWA2:* 270; *CWB1:* 54, 199–200; *CWB2:* 358, 390

Golenko, Valentina *CWPS:* 184

Golos, Jacob *CWA1:* 134

Gomulka, Wladyslaw *CWA2:* 193–94

Goncz, H. E. Arpad *CWB2:* 253

Good Neighbor policy *CWA2:* 265

Goodwin, Richard *CWPS:* 258

Gopkalo, Pantelei Yefimovich *CWB1:* 147

Gorbachev, Andrei Moiseyevich *CWB1:* 147–48

Gorbachev, Mikhail *CWA2:* 351 (ill.), 354 (ill.), 363 (ill.); *CWB1:* 120 (ill.), 146 (ill.), **146–58**, 156 (ill.); *CWB2:* 397 (ill.); *CWPS:* 286 (ill.), 291 (ill.), 294 (ill.), 299 (ill.), 305 (ill.), 308 (ill.), 310 (ill.)

"Address to the 43rd United Nations General Assembly Session, December 7, 1988" *CWPS:* 290, 294, **298–306**

Afghanistan and *CWA2:* 355–56; *CWB1:* 156; *CWB2:* 420; *CWPS:* 284, 294

Andropov, Yuri, and *CWB1:* 152–53; *CWB2:* 417

"At Historic Crossroads: Documents on the December 1989 Malta Summit" *CWPS:* 307–18

Baltic States and *CWPS:* 317–18

Brezhnev, Leonid, and *CWB1:* 152

Bush, George, and *CWA2:* 347, 356–57, 362–64, 368, 369, 372; *CWB1:* 57, 58, 157; *CWB2:* 405; *CWPS:* 283, 294–97, 300, 303–4, 305, 307–18

capitalism and *CWA2:* 352

Castro, Fidel, and *CWB1:* 91

Cheney, Richard, and *CWPS:* 305

Chernobyl disaster and *CWB1:* 153

China and *CWA2:* 356; *CWPS:* 294, 313

communism and *CWA2:* 352, 358; *CWB1:* 150; *CWB2:* 418, 422

Communist Party and *CWA2:* 347, 360–62, 367–68, 372; *CWB1:* 146, 150, 151, 152–53, 153–54, 157, 166; *CWB2:* 418, 419; *CWPS:* 296, 315

Conference on Security and Cooperation in Europe and *CWB2:* 265

Conventional Force Talks in Europe and *CWA2:* 355

coup attempt on *CWA2:* 368–69; *CWB1:* 58, 157; *CWB2:* 419, 422; *CWPS:* 296, 320

Cuba and *CWB1:* 91

democracy and *CWA2:* 347; *CWB1:* 154; *CWB2:* 418; *CWPS:* 290, 299, 301

disarmament and *CWPS:* 286, 287–96, 299–300, 302–4, 305–6, 308, 314

early life of *CWB1:* 147–51

East Germany and *CWA2:* 358–59; *CWB1:* 58; *CWPS:* 230

Eastern Bloc and *CWB2:* 421–22

economy and *CWA2:* 362; *CWB1:* 56, 154–55, 157; *CWB2:* 395, 414, 418, 442; *CWPS:* 283–85, 296, 299, 300, 301, 302, 308, 313, 315

education of *CWB1:* 148–51

elections of *CWA2:* 350–51, 373; *CWB1:* 45, 152–53, 157, 166; *CWB2:* 418; *CWPS:* 265, 283, 304–5

espionage and *CWA1:* 157

Estonia and *CWA2:* 361–62

freedom and *CWPS:* 283, 290, 296, 299, 308, 314–15

freedom of religion and *CWA2:* 357

as general secretary *CWB1:* 153–57, 166

Germany and *CWB1:* 58; *CWB2:* 405; *CWPS:* 317

glasnost and *CWA2:* 348, 351, 367; *CWB1:* 56, 146, 153; *CWB2:* 274, 395, 414, 416, 418

governmental reform by *CWB1:* 153–54

Great Terror and *CWB1:* 147–48

Gromyko, Andrey, and *CWB1:* 154, 166

honors for *CWB1:* 149–50, 157; *CWB2:* 421; *CWPS:* 317

Intermediate-range Nuclear Force (INF) treaty and *CWA2:* 372; *CWPS:* 290, 293, 300, 302–3

Iraq and *CWA2:* 365

Japan and *CWPS:* 313

Kennan, George F., and *CWB2:* 216, 217, 396

Khrushchev, Nikita, and *CWB1:* 151

Kissinger, Henry, and *CWB2:* 266

Kohl, Helmut, and *CWB2:* 273, 274

Komsomol and *CWB1:* 150, 151

Lithuania and *CWA2:* 362, 367

marriage of *CWB1:* 151

Memoirs of *CWB1:* 147, 148, 149

military and *CWA2:* 355–56; *CWB1:* 57, 58; *CWPS:* 312–13, 314

Nobel Peace Prize for *CWA2:* 361

North Atlantic Treaty Organization (NATO) and *CWA2:* 363–64

nuclear weapons and *CWA2:* 351, 352–55, 356–57, 364, 368, 369–70, 372; *CWB1:* 56, 58, 154–55; *CWB2:* 395–96, 418; *CWPS:* 265–66, 284–92, 293, 295, 299–300, 302–4, 308, 314, 319

peace and *CWPS:* 294, 298–99, 300–302, 314

perestroika and *CWA2:* 348, 351, 361; *CWB1:* 56, 121, 146, 153; *CWB2:* 395, 414, 416, 418; *CWPS:* 300–301, 302, 312–13

Persian Gulf War and *CWB2:* 421

Poland and *CWA2:* 358

Reagan, Ronald, and *CWA2:* 352–56, 372; *CWB1:* 56, 57, 155–56; *CWB2:* 395–96, 418; *CWPS:* 265–66, 282–92, 293–94, 295, 300, 303, 312

resignation of *CWA2:* 370; *CWB1:* 146, 157; *CWPS:* 296, 317, 319, 325

retirement of *CWB1:* 157

Sakharov, Andrey, and *CWB1:* 155; *CWB2:* 414

Shevardnadze, Eduard, and *CWA2:* 351; *CWB1:* 151, 154, 166; *CWB2:* 395, 418

Shultz, George, and *CWA2:* 352; *CWPS:* 283, 300, 303

Soviet collapse and *CWA2:* 367–69, 370, 372

Soviet republics and *CWA2:* 361–62, 367–68, 369, 370, 372

Stalin, Joseph, and *CWB1:* 150

Strategic Arms Reduction Talks (START) and *CWA2:* 357, 372

Strategic Defense Initiative (SDI) and *CWA2:* 352, 354; *CWB1:* 155; *CWB2:* 395–96; *CWPS:* 285, 287–92

Thatcher, Margaret, and *CWA2:* 352; *CWB2:* 442

Third World and *CWPS:* 283–84

United Nations and *CWA2:* 355, 365; *CWB1:* 156

World War II and *CWB1:* 148

Yeltsin, Boris, and *CWA2:* 367–68, 373; *CWB1:* 157; *CWB2:* 418, 419

Gorbachev, Raisa *CWB1:* 120 (ill.), 151–52, 153, 156 (ill.), 157

Gordievsky, Oleg *CWA1:* 157

Gore, Al *CWB1:* 61

Gorton, John Grey *CWPS:* 269

Gottwald, Klement *CWA1:* 34–35

Goulart, João Belchio Marques *CWA2:* 264

Gouzenko, Igor *CWA1:* 133–34, 135

Government Operations Committee *CWA1:* 118; *CWB2:* 334; *CWPS:* 171–72

Grand Alliance *CWA1:* 8–18. *See also* Big Three

Great Britain. *See also* British Commonwealth of Nations; British Empire
Acheson, Dean G., and *CWB1:* 2
Attlee, Clement R., and *CWB1:* 25, 27–32
Berlin airlift and *CWA1:* 62–65
Bevin, Ernest, and *CWB1:* 33, 35–40
Big Three and *CWA1:* 2, 9–10, 13
Bretton Woods Conference and *CWA1:* 12
Chamberlain, Neville, and *CWB1:* 27
China and *CWB1:* 39; *CWB2:* 307
colonialism and *CWA2:* 202, 206; *CWB2:* 309–10
Conservative Party in *CWB1:* 25, 27, 102; *CWB2:* 304, 439, 443
Dockers' Union in *CWB1:* 34
Dominican Republic and *CWB1:* 203
economy of *CWA1:* 17; *CWB1:* 28–29, 32, 38, 39, 170; *CWB2:* 305–6, 308–9, 310, 439–40; *CWPS:* 58
Egypt and *CWA2:* 202, 203
elections in *CWA1:* 15; *CWB1:* 36, 40; *CWB2:* 304, 305, 306, 308, 437; *CWPS:* 16
espionage and *CWA1:* 127, 131, 136–38, 140–44, 145–46, 151–52, 157
European Common Market and *CWB2:* 308–9
France and *CWB2:* 308

Germany and *CWA1:* 58–59
Grand Alliance and *CWA1:* 8–9
Greece and *CWA1:* 23; *CWB1:* 29, 38, 112; *CWPS:* 32, 34, 37
Grenada and *CWA2:* 341
Independent Labour Party in *CWB1:* 26
intelligence and *CWA1:* 127
Iran and *CWA1:* 20; *CWPS:* 12
Israel and *CWB1:* 36–37
Johnson, Lyndon B., and *CWB1:* 203
Jordan and *CWA2:* 204
Kurchatov, Igor, and *CWB2:* 291
labor in *CWB1:* 34
Labour Party in *CWB1:* 25, 27
Lend-Lease program and *CWB1:* 170
Liberal Party in *CWB1:* 102
Marshall Plan and *CWPS:* 48, 58
Middle East and *CWA2:* 202
missiles and *CWB2:* 307
Molotov, Vyacheslav, and *CWB2:* 348–49
nationalization in *CWB1:* 28–29
North Atlantic Treaty Organization and *CWB2:* 441–42
nuclear energy and *CWB2:* 284, 291
nuclear weapons and *CWA1:* 138; *CWA2:* 245–46, 373; *CWB1:* 31, 38, 108; *CWB2:* 307, 309, 440–41
Palestine and *CWB1:* 36–37
Reagan, Ronald, and *CWB2:* 441–42
Republic of China and *CWB2:* 307

socialism in *CWB1:* 25, 28–29; *CWB2:* 439–40; *CWPS:* 16
Soviet Union and *CWA1:* 18–19; *CWB1:* 35, 36–37, 108; *CWB2:* 307–8, 348–49, 437–38
Suez War and *CWA2:* 203; *CWB1:* 131–32, 142; *CWB2:* 306
Turkey and *CWA1:* 23; *CWB1:* 29, 38, 112; *CWPS:* 32, 34–35, 38
United States of America and *CWPS:* 21–22, 25–26, 28–29
Vietnam and *CWB1:* 141
West Germany and *CWB2:* 308
Western European Union (WEU) and *CWA1:* 37
World War II and *CWA1:* 2, 3, 8–11, 12, 13, 15, 17, 86; *CWA2:* 364; *CWB1:* 35, 100, 102–7; *CWB2:* 219, 348–49, 438; *CWPS:* 16–17

Great Depression *CWA1:* 5, 103–4
Byrnes, James F., and *CWB1:* 64
Carter, Jimmy, and *CWB1:* 71–72
Federal Bureau of Investigation and *CWB1:* 188–89
Johnson, Lyndon B., and *CWB1:* 195–96
MacArthur, Douglas, and *CWB2:* 294–95
Marshall, George C., and *CWB2:* 323
New Deal and *CWB2:* 455
Oppenheimer, J. Robert, and *CWB2:* 369–70
Roosevelt, Franklin D., and *CWB1:* 64; *CWB2:* 295, 389

Great Leap Forward *CWA2:* 206; *CWB1:* 118–19; *CWB2:* 317–18, 470–71

H

I

CWB2: 435. See also Israel

Jiang Qing *CWB1:* 119; *CWB2:* 320

Jiang Zemin *CWB1:* 121, 122

Jimmy Carter Library *CWB1:* 80

Job Corps *CWA2:* 282

Joe-1 *CWA1:* 89–90; *CWB2:* 410

Joe-4 *CWA1:* 95

John Paul II (pope) *CWA2:* 357

Johnson, Lady Bird *CWB1:* 195

Johnson, Louis *CWA1:* 95

Johnson, Lyndon B. *CWA2:* 261 (ill.), 272 (ill.); *CWB1:* 7 (ill.), 194 (ill.), **194–205,** 199 (ill.); *CWB2:* 222 (ill.), 281 (ill.); *CWPS:* 263–64

Acheson, Dean G., and *CWB1:* 7–8

Alliance for Progress and *CWA2:* 263

character of *CWB1:* 196

China and *CWB1:* 201

civil rights and *CWB1:* 194, 196, 197, 198; *CWB2:* 222

Clifford, Clark M., and *CWB1:* 109, 113, 114

communism and *CWA2:* 270, 283; *CWB1:* 201

containment and *CWB1:* 198

death of *CWB1:* 204–5

Dominican Republic and *CWB1:* 203

early life of *CWB1:* 195–96

election of *CWA2:* 270; *CWB1:* 199–200

espionage and *CWB1:* 203

Goldwater, Barry, and *CWB1:* 199–200

Great Britain and *CWB1:* 203

Great Depression and *CWB1:* 195–96

Great Society of *CWA2:* 254, 272, 282; *CWB1:* 197–98, 201

Harriman, W. Averell, and *CWB1:* 174–75

health care and *CWB1:* 198

Ho Chi Minh and *CWB1:* 182

Kennedy, John F., and *CWB1:* 197; *CWB2:* 221, 228

Kissinger, Henry, and *CWB2:* 257

Kleberg, Richard, and *CWB1:* 195

Kosygin, Aleksey, and *CWA2:* 247; *CWB2:* 281

Latin America and *CWA2:* 263–65

MacArthur, Douglas, and *CWB2:* 302

McNamara, Robert S., and *CWB2:* 337, 342

North Korea and *CWB1:* 203

nuclear weapons and *CWA2:* 247, 258; *CWB1:* 204

Oppenheimer, J. Robert, and *CWB2:* 377

Panama and *CWA2:* 263

peace and *CWB1:* 200, 204

poverty and *CWB1:* 195, 197–98, 201

Rayburn, Sam, and *CWB1:* 195

retirement of *CWB1:* 204

Rusk, Dean, and *CWB1:* 201, 202

Six-Day War and *CWB1:* 203

Soviet Union and *CWB2:* 281

Strategic Arms Limitation Talks and *CWB1:* 204

in U.S. Congress *CWB1:* 196

vice presidency of *CWB1:* 197

Vietnam War and *CWA2:* 270, 271–73, 282, 283, 289–90; *CWB1:* 7–8, 109, 114, 174–75, 182, 183, 194, 198–203, 203–4; *CWB2:* 281, 302, 342, 358, 359

World War II and *CWB1:* 196

Joliot-Curie Medal *CWB2:* 291

Jordan *CWA1:* 161; *CWA2:* 204; *CWB1:* 29, 203; *CWB2:* 307

Jornada del Muerto CWA1: 79

Junta de Energía Nuclear (JEN) *CWA2:* 242–43

K

Kádár, János *CWA2:* 196, 358; *CWB2:* 239 (ill.)

Kaganovich, Lazar *CWB2:* 231–32, 234, 236

Kassem, Abdul Karim *CWA2:* 204

Kazakhstan *CWA2:* 370, 373

Keenan, Joseph B. *CWB1:* 190 (ill.)

Keep, John L. *CWB1:* 41

Keeping Faith: Memoirs of a President CWB1: 79–80

Kennan, George F. *CWA1:* 19 (ill.), 19–20, 35–36; *CWA2:* 356; *CWB2:* 207 (ill.), **207–17,** 214 (ill.), 396; *CWPS:* 6 (ill.), 13 (ill.)

containment and *CWPS:* 4, 9, 13, 14, 62, 72

"Long Telegram" and *CWPS:* 3–4, **5–15,** 18, 25, 26

Marshall Plan and *CWPS:* 43

NSC-68 and *CWPS:* 76–77

nuclear weapons and *CWPS:* 72

propaganda and *CWPS:* 10

threats and *CWPS:* 10, 12

Truman Doctrine and *CWPS:* 41

World War II and *CWPS:* 13–14

Kennan Institute for Advanced Russian Studies *CWB2:* 208

Kennedy, Ethel *CWPS:* 258

Kennedy, Jacqueline "Jackie" Lee Bouvier *CWB2:* 220, 221

Kennedy, John F. *CWA2:* 227 (ill.), 229 (ill.), 230 (ill.), 259 (ill.), 261 (ill.); *CWB1:* 112 (ill.), 174 (ill.); *CWB2:* 218 (ill.), **218–29,** 222 (ill.), 224 (ill.), 228 (ill.), 340 (ill.); *CWPS:* 209 (ill.), 211 (ill.), 226 (ill.), 229 (ill.), 230 (ill.), 237 (ill.), 239 (ill.), 240 (ill.), 245 (ill.), 260 (ill.)

Acheson, Dean G., and *CWB1:* 7

Adenauer, Konrad, and *CWB1:* 15

Alliance for Progress and *CWA2:* 262–63

as author *CWB2:* 219

Bay of Pigs and *CWA2:* 217, 218, 258–59; *CWB1:* 87, 144; *CWB2:* 223, 340; *CWPS:* 233

Berlin and *CWA1:* 72–73, 76–77; *CWA2:* 259–60; *CWPS:* 207, 208–15, 224–31

Berlin Wall and *CWB1:* 15; *CWB2:* 218, 226, 275; *CWPS:* 207, 224–31

brinkmanship and *CWA2:* 256

Bundy, McGeorge, and *CWPS:* 236

China and *CWA2:* 266

Churchill, Winston, and *CWB1:* 101

Civil Defense and *CWPS:* 212–13, 215

civil rights and *CWB2:* 218, 221–22

Clifford, Clark M., and *CWB1:* 113

communism and *CWA2:* 251–54, 262, 269; *CWB2:* 340

containment and *CWPS:* 263

Cuba and *CWB1:* 87, 88

Cuban Missile Crisis and *CWA2:* 213–14, 221–27, 228, 229, 260; *CWB1:* 7, 89–91; *CWB2:* 218, 226–28, 238, 308; *CWPS:* 192, 234–35, 236–37, 238–39, 241–42, 244–51, 253–61

death of *CWA2:* 254, 270; *CWB1:* 113, 194, 197; *CWB2:* 218, 222, 228–29

Dulles, John Foster, and *CWB1:* 131

early life of *CWB2:* 218–19, 230–31

election of *CWA1:* 70; *CWA2:* 212, 251; *CWB1:* 113, 197; *CWB2:* 220, 221, 358, 390; *CWPS:* 191, 209

espionage and *CWA1:* 152

on freedom *CWPS:* 228–29

Germany and *CWPS:* 210

Gromyko, Andrey, and *CWA2:* 224–25

Harriman, W. Averell, and *CWB1:* 173

honors for *CWB2:* 219

Hoover, J. Edgar, and *CWA1:* 109; *CWB1:* 192

"I am a Berliner" speech of *CWPS:* 207, **224–31**

imperialism and *CWB1:* 87, 88; *CWB2:* 223, 226

inaugural address of *CWB2:* 222

Johnson, Lyndon B., and *CWB1:* 197; *CWB2:* 221, 228

Kennan, George F., and *CWB2:* 215

Khrushchev, Nikita, and *CWA1:* 70–71; *CWA2:* 226, 228, 251–54, 259–61; *CWB2:* 223–26, 227–28, 230; *CWPS:* 192, 207, 209–11, 214–15, 217–18, 219–21, 235, 244–45, 253–61

Kissinger, Henry, and *CWB2:* 256, 257

Macmillan, Harold, and *CWB2:* 225, 308–9

McCarthy, Joseph R., and *CWB2:* 220

McNamara, Robert S., and *CWA2:* 253; *CWB2:* 337, 339–40, 341

military and *CWA2:* 256; *CWB2:* 225

nation building and *CWA1:* 177

North Atlantic Treaty Organization and *CWPS:* 211

nuclear war and *CWPS:* 212–13, 214

nuclear weapons and *CWA2:* 246, 256–58; *CWB2:* 226–27, 227–28, 341

Operation Mongoose and *CWA2:* 219; *CWB1:* 88; *CWB2:* 226

Oppenheimer, J. Robert, and *CWB2:* 377

peace and *CWB2:* 221; *CWPS:* 213–14, 246–47, 248–49

Peace Corps and *CWA2:* 255; *CWB2:* 221

"Radio and Television Report to the American People on the Berlin Crisis, July 25, 1961" *CWPS:* 208–16

"Radio and Television Report to the American People on the Soviet Arms Buildup in Cuba, October 22, 1962" *CWPS:* 244–52

disarmament and *CWPS:* 195, 197, 201, 219

domino theory and *CWPS:* 221–22

Dulles, John Foster, and *CWPS:* 220

East Germany and *CWB2:* 224–25; *CWPS:* 207, 208, 210

Eastern Bloc and *CWA2:* 193–96

economy and *CWA2:* 292; *CWB2:* 239; *CWPS:* 120, 189–90

education of *CWPS:* 174, 175

Eisenhower, Dwight D., and *CWA1:* 185–88; *CWA2:* 193, 200–201, 205, 210–12, 240; *CWB1:* 141, 144; *CWB2:* 230, 237, 238, 308; *CWPS:* 188–89, 191–92, 195, 197, 200–201, 202, 209

election of *CWA1:* 52; *CWA2:* 196–97; *CWB1:* 150–51; *CWPS:* 99, 187–88

espionage and *CWA2:* 240; *CWB1:* 144; *CWB2:* 238, 308; *CWPS:* 202

Fanfani, Amintore, and *CWPS:* 220

as first secretary *CWB2:* 233–39

freedom and *CWB2:* 233, 234

Garst, Roswell, and *CWPS:* 197, 199

Germany and *CWPS:* 221

Gorbachev, Mikhail, and *CWB1:* 151

Great Terror and *CWB2:* 232, 236; *CWPS:* 175, 176–83

Gromyko, Andrey, and *CWB1:* 162, 164; *CWPS:* 217

Harriman, W. Averell, and *CWB1:* 171

housing and *CWPS:* 189–90

Hungary and *CWA2:* 195–96; *CWB2:* 236; *CWPS:* 182

Kaganovich, Lazar, and *CWB2:* 231–32, 234, 236

Kennedy, John F., and *CWA1:* 70–71; *CWA2:* 226, 228, 251–54, 259–61; *CWB2:* 223–26, 227–28, 230; *CWPS:* 192, 207, 209–11, 214–15, 217–18, 219–21, 235, 244–45, 253–61

KGB (Soviet secret police) and *CWB1:* 46; *CWB2:* 240; *CWPS:* 199

Khrushchev, Sergei, on *CWPS:* 175, 184–94, 199, 250, 256

"Khrushchev's Secret Speech on the Berlin Crisis, August 1961" *CWPS:* 217–23

"kitchen debate" and *CWB2:* 237 (ill.), 238, 357

Kosygin, Aleksey, and *CWB2:* 280

Kurchatov, Igor, and *CWB2:* 290–91

Limited Test-Ban Treaty of 1963 *CWB2:* 238–39

Macmillan, Harold, and *CWA2:* 191; *CWB2:* 307, 308; *CWPS:* 220

Malenkov, Georgy M., and *CWB2:* 233, 234, 236; *CWPS:* 120, 175

Mao Zedong and *CWA2:* 265–66

McCloy, John J., and *CWPS:* 214, 217, 219–20, 221

military and *CWB2:* 239–40; *CWPS:* 175, 190–91, 193–94, 202, 211, 214–15, 221

Molotov, Vyacheslav, and *CWB2:* 234, 236, 352–53

nation building and *CWA1:* 177; *CWA2:* 325

Nixon, Richard M., and *CWB2:* 238, 357; *CWPS:* 195

nuclear energy and *CWA2:* 241

nuclear war and *CWPS:* 192, 198–99, 214, 218, 220

nuclear weapons and *CWA1:* 70, 174–75; *CWA2:* 200–201; *CWB1:* 144; *CWB2:* 227–28, 235, 238–39, 411; *CWPS:* 120, 175, 190–91, 220

peace and *CWB2:* 352; *CWPS:* 175, 187–88, 192, 195–203, 256, 258, 260

"Peace and Progress Must Triumph in Our Time" speech of *CWPS:* 175, **195–203**

Penkovsky, Oleg, and *CWA1:* 151

Poland and *CWA2:* 193–94

propaganda and *CWPS:* 203

reconnaissance and *CWA1:* 150

religion and *CWB2:* 234

removal of *CWA2:* 254–55

retirement of *CWB2:* 240

Rockefeller, Nelson A., and *CWPS:* 188

Sakharov, Andrey, and *CWB2:* 411

space race and *CWB2:* 235

Stalin, Joseph, and *CWA1:* 188; *CWA2:* 192–93, 265–66, 292; *CWB1:* 46, 118; *CWB2:* 230, 231–32, 233, 236, 291, 352, 419, 435–36, 471; *CWPS:* 174–75, 176–83

strength and *CWA1:* 70

Third World and *CWA2:* 210

threats and *CWA1:* 69–71; *CWPS:* 214–15, 219–21, 234

Tito, Josip Broz, and
CWB2: 448–49
U-2 aircraft and *CWA2:*
211–12
Ulbricht, Walter, and
CWA1: 71, 73; *CWPS:*
207, 208, 209, 210, 215,
217, 224, 226–27
United Nations and
CWA2: 191, 210;
CWB2: 233–34, 238
Virgin Land program and
CWB2: 238
West Berlin and *CWB1:*
132; *CWB2:* 224–25,
235–37
World War II and *CWB2:*
233; *CWPS:* 174, 187
Yeltsin, Boris, and *CWB2:*
419
Zhou Enlai and *CWB2:*
471
Khrushchev, Nina Petrovna
CWPS: 184, 195
Khrushchev, Sergei *CWPS:*
175, **184–94,** 185 (ill.),
199, 250, 256
**"Khrushchev's Secret
Speech on the Berlin
Crisis, August 1961"**
CWPS: 217–23
Kim Il Sung *CWA1:* 45, 46;
CWB2: 241 (ill.),
241–48; *CWPS:* 62, 77,
79
Kim Jong Il *CWB2:* 248
King, Martin Luther, Jr.
CWA1: 109; *CWA2:*
277, 279–81, 282 (ill.),
282; *CWB1:* 192, 204;
CWPS: 133
Kirkpatrick, Jeane *CWA2:*
339, 341; *CWB2:* 249
(ill.), **249–54,** 252 (ill.)
Kissinger, Henry *CWA2:*
303 (ill.); *CWB2:* 255
(ill.), **255–67,** 259 (ill.),
261 (ill.); *CWPS:* 264,
271–72, 274–75, 280
Acheson, Dean G., and
CWB1: 8
Allende, Salvador, and
CWB2: 263–64

as author *CWB2:* 255, 256
Brezhnev, Leonid, and
CWB2: 261–62
Bush, George, and *CWA2:*
356; *CWB2:* 266
Camp David Accords and
CWB2: 263
Carter, Jimmy, and
CWB2: 266
Chile and *CWA2:* 308;
CWB2: 263–64
China and *CWA2:*
300–301, 302; *CWB2:*
255, 260, 360, 470
Council on Foreign Rela-
tions and *CWB2:* 256
détente and *CWA2:* 310,
311, 315; *CWB2:* 255,
260–62, 264, 390
early life of *CWB2:*
255–56
Ford, Gerald, and *CWA2:*
314; *CWB2:* 264–65
as foreign affairs consul-
tant *CWB2:* 256–57, 266
Gorbachev, Mikhail, and
CWB2: 266
Helsinki Accords and
CWB2: 264, 265–66
honors for *CWB2:* 255,
259–60
human rights and *CWB2:*
264
imperialism and *CWB2:*
263–64
Johnson, Lyndon B., and
CWB2: 257
Kennedy, John F., and
CWB2: 256, 257
as lecturer *CWB2:* 256
mutual assured destruc-
tion and *CWB2:*
260–61
as national security advisor *CWB2:* 257–65
National Security Council
and *CWB2:* 257
Nixon, Richard M., and
CWB2: 257, 259,
261–62, 262–63, 359
nuclear weapons and
CWA2: 305; *CWB2:*
256, 260–62

October War and *CWB2:*
262–63, 363
Palestine and *CWA2:* 328
Reagan, Ronald, and
CWB2: 266, 390
Republic of China and
CWB2: 260
reputation of *CWB2:* 258,
263, 264–65, 266
Rockefeller, Nelson A.,
and *CWB2:* 256
as secretary of state
CWB2: 262–66
Soviet Union and *CWA2:*
302–3, 304; *CWB2:*
255, 260–62, 264
Strategic Arms Limitation
Talks and *CWB2:* 261
U.S. Congress and *CWB2:*
264
Vietnam War and *CWA2:*
312; *CWB2:* 255,
257–60, 261–62, 264,
359
Vietnamization and
CWB2: 258
Watergate scandal and
CWB2: 363
World War II and *CWB2:*
255–56
Zhou Enlai and *CWA2:*
301; *CWB2:* 470
"Kitchen debate" *CWB2:*
237 (ill.), 238, 357
Kleberg, Richard *CWB1:* 195
Klock, Augustus *CWB2:* 368
Kohl, Hans *CWB2:* 269
Kohl, Helmut *CWA2:* 356,
364; *CWB1:* 58; *CWB2:*
268 (ill.), **268–76**
Komsomol
Andropov, Yuri, and
CWB1: 45
Brezhnev, Leonid, and
CWB1: 42
Gorbachev, Mikhail, and
CWB1: 150, 151
Kosygin, Aleksey, and
CWB2: 278
Shevardnadze, Eduard,
and *CWB2:* 417
Koo, Wellington *CWPS:* 67
Korbel, Josef *CWB2:* 403

Korea *CWA1:* 45–46; *CWB2:* 241–42, 243, 244, 297–98; *CWPS:* 77, 79. *See also* Korean War; North Korea; South Korea

Korean Airlines tragedy *CWA2:* 343; *CWB2:* 246, 394

Korean War *CWA1:* 47 (ill.), 50 (ill.)

Acheson, Dean G., and *CWB1:* 5

Attlee, Clement R., and *CWB1:* 32

beginning of *CWA1:* 28, 46; *CWB2:* 434

Bevin, Ernest, and *CWB1:* 40

Byrnes, James F., and *CWB1:* 68

Chiang Kai-shek and *CWB1:* 98

China and *CWA1:* 46, 47, 48; *CWB1:* 5, 98; *CWB2:* 243–44, 299–300, 469; *CWPS:* 63, 80–81, 84, 86

conduct of *CWA1:* 45–48; *CWB1:* 5

death in *CWA1:* 48; *CWA2:* 372; *CWPS:* 324

definition of *CWA1:* 28

Eisenhower, Dwight D., and *CWB1:* 134, 140, 143; *CWPS:* 106–7, 108

end of *CWA1:* 48, 169; *CWB2:* 244; *CWPS:* 86, 97, 110

espionage and *CWA1:* 143

implications of *CWA1:* 48–52

Kim Il Sung and *CWB2:* 243–44; *CWPS:* 62, 77

MacArthur, Douglas, and *CWB1:* 5, 40; *CWB2:* 243, 293, 299–301, 327, 461; *CWPS:* 62–63, 80–81, 84–85

Mao Zedong and *CWB2:* 299

Marshall, George C., and *CWB2:* 327

nuclear weapons and *CWA1:* 47, 48; *CWPS:* 63, 80–81

peace and *CWPS:* 106–7, 108

Roosevelt, Eleanor, on *CWPS:* 91, 94

Rusk, Dean, and *CWB1:* 202

Soviet Union and *CWB1:* 5; *CWPS:* 77, 108

Truman, Harry S., and *CWB1:* 5, 98, 139–40; *CWB2:* 299–301, 461; *CWPS:* 62–63, 77, 79–80, 86, 101, 110

United Nations and *CWB1:* 5; *CWB2:* 243, 299; *CWPS:* 79–80, 90–91, 94, 97

Zhou Enlai and *CWB2:* 469

Korean Workers' Party *CWB2:* 242, 247

Kosygin, Aleksey *CWA2:* 247, 255–56; *CWB1:* 46; *CWB2:* 277 (ill.), **277–82**, 281 (ill.)

Ku Klux Klan *CWA1:* 109; *CWB1:* 63, 192

Kubrick, Stanley *CWA2:* 236

Kung, H. H. *CWA1:* 40 (ill.)

Kurchatov, Igor *CWA1:* 81, 89–90, 91; *CWA2:* 244–45; *CWB2:* 283 (ill.), **283–92**, 290 (ill.), 373, 410–11, 433

Kurchatov, Marina *CWA1:* 90

Kuwait *CWA2:* 365; *CWB1:* 60; *CWB2:* 421; *CWPS:* 317

L

La Follette, Robert M., Jr. *CWB2:* 331

Labor *CWA1:* 6, 104, 108; *CWA2:* 193–94, 357–58; *CWB1:* 34, 35; *CWPS:* 128–29, 131, 132, 149, 158

Labor camps *CWA1:* 120–21

Labour Party *CWA1:* 15; *CWB1:* 25, 27

Laika *CWA2:* 196

Laird, Melvin R. *CWB2:* 261 (ill.)

Lamphere, Robert *CWA1:* 135, 136–37, 138 (ill.)

Laos *CWA1:* 181–82

Latin America *CWB1:* 76; *CWB2:* 327, 361–62

Alliance for Progress and *CWA2:* 252, 262–63

Carter, Jimmy, and *CWA2:* 324

composition of *CWA2:* 193, 261, 324

democracy and *CWA2:* 262, 263, 339

dictatorship and *CWA2:* 308, 324, 330–31, 339–40

Good Neighbor policy in *CWA2:* 265

human rights and *CWA2:* 324

imperialism in *CWA1:* 36; *CWA2:* 261–65

Johnson, Lyndon B., and *CWA2:* 263–65

military and *CWA2:* 263

Monroe Doctrine and *CWA1:* 187

nation building and *CWA1:* 179–80; *CWA2:* 261–65, 339–41

nuclear weapons and *CWA2:* 248

Reagan, Ronald, and *CWA2:* 339–41

Roosevelt, Franklin D., and *CWA2:* 265

Latin American Nuclear-Free Zone Treaty *CWA2:* 248, 258, 265

Latvia *CWA2:* 369

Le Duc Tho *CWB2:* 259 (ill.), 260

League for the Independence of Vietnam. *See* Vietminh

League of Nations *CWB1:* 126, 127; *CWPS:* 20, 90, 92

Leahy, William *CWA1:* 25
Lebanon *CWA2:* 204; *CWB1:* 132; *CWB2:* 307
Lee, Andrew Daulton *CWA1:* 154–55
Legion of Honor *CWB2:* 377
LeMay, Curtis E. *CWA1:* 93, 93 (ill.); *CWA2:* 237–38
Lend-Lease program *CWB1:* 2, 170, 171
Lenin, Vladimir I. *CWA1:* 4 (ill.), 7 (ill.), 102 (ill.); *CWB2:* 428 (ill.); *CWPS:* 295 (ill.)
  Allende, Salvador, and *CWB1:* 18
  Bolshevik Revolution and *CWA1:* 3, 6; *CWB1:* 159; *CWB2:* 278, 347, 427
  communism and *CWB1:* 179; *CWB2:* 312; *CWPS:* 64, 127–28, 128–29
  Communist Party and *CWA1:* 3, 101; *CWB1:* 159; *CWPS:* 2
  death of *CWA1:* 7; *CWB2:* 381, 428–29
  government of *CWA1:* 7
  Mao Zedong and *CWPS:* 64
  Marxism and *CWA1:* 6
  Molotov, Vyacheslav, and *CWB2:* 347
  morality and *CWPS:* 284
  Stalin, Joseph, and *CWB2:* 427, 428–29; *CWPS:* 178
  tomb of *CWA2:* 355
Leningraders *CWA1:* 121
Levine, Isaac Don *CWPS:* 62, **64–70,** 66 (ill.), 81
Li Peng *CWB2:* 465
Liberal Party *CWB1:* 102
Liberty. *See* Freedom
Libya *CWB2:* 398–99
Lilienthal, David *CWA1:* 93–94, 94 (ill.), 95
Limited Test-Ban Treaty of 1963 *CWA2:* 234, 244, 247, 261; *CWB1:* 91,

173; *CWB2:* 227–28, 238–39, 309; *CWPS:* 261
Lin Sen *CWA1:* 40 (ill.)
Lippmann, Walter *CWA1:* 3
Listening devices *CWA1:* 137
Listening stations *CWA1:* 144–45
Lithuania *CWA2:* 362, 367, 369
Little Boy *CWA1:* 85, 86 (ill.), 86–87, 88
The Little Red Book CWB2: 318
Liu Bocheng *CWB1:* 119
Lock picks *CWA1:* 136
Lockheed Corporation *CWA1:* 147
Lodge, Henry Cabot *CWB2:* 221; *CWPS:* 200
Long March *CWB1:* 94, 117; *CWB2:* 316, 466–67
Long Peace *CWA2:* 374
"Long Telegram" *CWA1:* 19–20; *CWB2:* 210–12; *CWPS:* **5–15**
  containment and *CWPS:* 3–4
  excerpt from *CWPS:* 5–14
  Iran occupation and *CWPS:* 23
  isolationism and *CWPS:* 41
  "Novikov Telegram" and *CWPS:* 25
  on propaganda *CWPS:* 10
  strength and *CWPS:* 18, 26
  on threats *CWPS:* 10
Looking Forward CWB1: 61
"The Looking Glass" *CWPS:* 175, **184–94**
Los Alamos National Laboratory *CWA1:* 85 (ill.); *CWB2:* 285, 287, 368, 371, 409
  hydrogen bombs and *CWA1:* 95
  management of *CWA1:* 92
  Manhattan Project and *CWA1:* 83–85, 87, 90

Los Arzamas *CWA1:* 89–90
Lossky, Nicolas O. *CWB2:* 381–82
Lovett, Robert A. *CWB2:* 338, 339
Loyalty programs *CWPS:* 130–31, 132, 163
  civil rights and *CWA1:* 107
  Red Scare and *CWA1:* 104, 107, 108, 112, 115, 171
  Stalin, Joseph, and *CWA1:* 120
Lucas, Scott *CWA1:* 117
Lumumba, Patrice *CWA1:* 176; *CWA2:* 193, 207, 208
Luxembourg *CWA1:* 37

M

MacArthur, Douglas *CWA1:* 29, 42, 46–47, 49 (ill.); *CWB2:* 293 (ill.), **293–302,** 296 (ill.), 300 (ill.), 301 (ill.); *CWPS:* 62–63, 68, 80 (ill.), 83 (ill.), 85 (ill.)
  as author *CWB2:* 302
  Bevin, Ernest, and *CWB1:* 40
  character of *CWB2:* 294, 298
  China and *CWB2:* 298–99, 299–300
  Civilian Conservation Corps and *CWB2:* 295
  communism and *CWB2:* 293
  containment and *CWB2:* 295, 297, 298, 299
  death of *CWB2:* 302
  early life of *CWB2:* 293–94
  Eisenhower, Dwight D., and *CWB1:* 135
  election of 1952 and *CWB2:* 301–2
  Great Depression and *CWB2:* 294–95

honors for *CWB2:* 294, 296–97

Japan and *CWB2:* 293, 295–97, 298, 299

Johnson, Lyndon B., and *CWB2:* 302

Korean War and *CWB1:* 5, 40; *CWB2:* 243, 293, 299–301, 327, 461

Marshall, George C., and *CWB2:* 327

McCarthy, Joseph R., and *CWB2:* 299–300

as military advisor *CWB2:* 295

"Old Soldiers Never Die; They Just Fade Away" speech *CWPS:* 79–87

Philippines and *CWB2:* 295, 302

retirement of *CWB2:* 302

Roosevelt, Franklin D., and *CWB2:* 296–97

South Korea and *CWB2:* 297–98

Syngman Rhee and *CWB2:* 297–98

Truman, Harry S., and *CWB1:* 5, 40; *CWB2:* 297, 298, 299–301, 327, 461

as U.S. Army chief of staff *CWB2:* 294–95

U.S. Congress and *CWB2:* 300–301

Vietnam War and *CWB2:* 302

World War I and *CWB2:* 294, 295

World War II and *CWB2:* 293, 295–97

Maclean, Donald *CWA1:* 128, 140, 142–43, 143 (ill.); *CWPS:* 50

Macmillan, Harold *CWA1:* 175 (ill.); *CWA2:* 191; *CWB2:* 225, 303 (ill.), 303–11, 309 (ill.); *CWPS:* 220

MAD. *See* Mutual assured destruction (MAD)

Malcolm X *CWA2:* 281

Malenkov, Georgy M. *CWA1:* 52, 169, 170 (ill.), 170–71; *CWB2:* 233, 234, 236; *CWPS:* 99, 101, 120, 175

Malta Summit *CWB2:* 405; *CWPS:* 307–18

"Man of the Year" award *CWA2:* 361

Mandela, Nelson *CWB1:* 91

Manhattan Project *CWPS:* 5, 73, 133

definition of *CWA1:* 80

development by *CWA1:* 9, 79–80, 83–84, 87, 135; *CWA2:* 244; *CWB1:* 31; *CWB2:* 285, 409, 458

espionage and *CWA1:* 88–89, 90–91, 115, 128, 138, 139; *CWB1:* 191–92; *CWB2:* 285, 287, 351

Federal Bureau of Investigation and *CWB1:* 191–92

hydrogen bombs and *CWB2:* 375

Oppenheimer, J. Robert, and *CWB2:* 366, 368, 370–72

testing by *CWA1:* 13–14, 80–81, 85–86, 87; *CWB2:* 285, 287, 458

Mao Zedong *CWA1:* 41 (ill.); *CWA2:* 267 (ill.), 303 (ill.); *CWB2:* 312 (ill.), **312–20**, 315 (ill.), 317 (ill.), 319 (ill.), 468 (ill.)

as author *CWB2:* 318–19

capitalism and *CWB2:* 313

children of *CWA1:* 48

civil war and *CWA1:* 39–42; *CWA2:* 327

communism and *CWB2:* 312, 314–15, 317–18, 319

Communist Party and *CWB2:* 313, 315, 317, 318, 467

"Crimes of Stalin" speech and *CWPS:* 182

Cultural Revolution of *CWA2:* 266–67, 276, 277, 293–95, 295 (ill.); *CWB1:* 119; *CWB2:* 246, 318–20, 471–72

Czechoslovakia and *CWA2:* 300

death of *CWA2:* 327; *CWB1:* 119; *CWB2:* 320, 472

Deng Xiaoping and *CWB1:* 118–19, 119–20

early life of *CWB2:* 313–15

economy and *CWB1:* 118–19

freedom and *CWB2:* 312, 314, 318, 320

Gang of Four and *CWB2:* 320

Great Leap Forward of *CWB1:* 118–19; *CWB2:* 317–18, 470–71

health of *CWB2:* 319–20

Ho Chi Minh and *CWB1:* 179

isolationism and *CWB1:* 116

Khrushchev, Nikita, and *CWA2:* 265–66

Kissinger, Henry, and *CWA2:* 301, 302

Korean War and *CWB2:* 299

Lenin, Vladimir I., and *CWPS:* 64

Long March and *CWB2:* 316, 466–67

Maoism of *CWB2:* 312–13

Marx, Karl, and *CWPS:* 64

Marxism and *CWB2:* 312, 314–15

May Fourth Movement and *CWB2:* 314

Nixon, Richard M., and *CWA2:* 301; *CWB2:* 313, 470; *CWPS:* 276

nuclear weapons and *CWA2:* 206

ping-pong and *CWA2:* 302

Red Scare and *CWA1:* 111
revolution and *CWB1:*
5–6, 93, 96, 117; *CWB2:*
243, 298–99, 313,
315–16, 324, 466–67;
CWPS: 61–62, 64
Sino-Soviet Treaty and
CWB2: 316–17; *CWPS:*
69
Soviet Union and *CWB2:*
313, 316–18; *CWPS:* 65
Stalin, Joseph, and *CWA1:*
40; *CWPS:* 65, 69
swimming and *CWB2:* 318
Truman, Harry S., and
CWA1: 40, 42
World War II and *CWB2:*
316
Zhou Enlai and *CWB2:*
470–72
Zhu De and *CWB2:* 316
Mao Zedong on People's War
CWB2: 318
Maoism *CWB2:* 312–13
March on Washington
CWA2: 279–80, 280
(ill.)
Marshall, George C. *CWB1:*
30 (ill.); *CWB2:* 321
(ill.), **321–28**, 326 (ill.),
468 (ill.); *CWPS:* 44 (ill.)
Berlin airlift and *CWB2:*
327
character of *CWB2:* 322
China and *CWA1:* 40–41;
CWB2: 324, 467;
CWPS: 65
Civilian Conservation
Corps and *CWB2:* 323
Clayton, Will, and *CWPS:*
43
containment and *CWB2:*
325
death of *CWB2:* 327
early life of *CWB2:* 321–22
economy and *CWB2:*
321, 324–26
as general *CWB2:* 321,
323–24
Germany and *CWPS:*
40–41
Great Depression and
CWB2: 323

Greece and *CWB2:* 326;
CWPS: 32, 34
honors for *CWB2:* 321,
324, 325, 327; *CWPS:*
43
Israel and *CWB2:* 326–27
Kennan, George F., and
CWB2: 212
Korea and *CWB2:* 243
Korean War and *CWB2:*
327
Latin America and *CWB2:*
327
as lecturer *CWB2:* 323
MacArthur, Douglas, and
CWB2: 327
Marshall Plan and
CWA1: 31; *CWB1:* 4,
113; *CWB2:* 324–25;
CWPS: 33, **43–51**
McCarthy, Joseph R., and
CWA1: 44, 117; *CWB2:*
324, 333–34; *CWPS:*
171
National Security Council
and *CWB2:* 324
North Atlantic Treaty Or-
ganization and *CWB2:*
327
Organization of American
States and *CWB2:* 327
Pershing, John J., and
CWB2: 322
Red Scare and *CWA1:* 44
replacement of *CWB1:*
138–39; *CWPS:* 100
retirement of *CWB2:* 327
Rio Pact and *CWB2:* 327
Roosevelt, Franklin D.,
and *CWB2:* 323
as secretary of defense
CWB2: 321, 327
as secretary of state
CWB1: 3, 68; *CWB2:*
321, 324–27
Soviet Union and *CWB2:*
324
Truman Doctrine and
CWA1: 23
Truman, Harry S., and
CWB2: 324, 326–27
Turkey and *CWB2:* 326;
CWPS: 32, 34

U.S. Congress and *CWB2:*
326
U.S. State Department and
CWB2: 324
World War I and *CWB2:*
322
World War II and *CWB2:*
323–24
Marshall Plan *CWA1:* 28,
31–32, 34, 67; *CWPS:*
43–51
Acheson, Dean G., and
CWB1: 4
Attlee, Clement R., and
CWB1: 30–31
Bevin, Ernest, and *CWB1:*
38
Cambridge Spies and
CWPS: 50
China and *CWPS:* 65–66
Clifford, Clark M., and
CWB1: 112–13
containment and *CWB1:*
112–13, 172; *CWPS:* 9,
44, 52–59, 61
Czechoslovakia and
CWPS: 48, 50
East Germany and *CWB2:*
272
Eastern Bloc and *CWB2:*
325; *CWPS:* 30, 48, 57
economy and *CWB1:* 4,
113; *CWPS:* 33, 43–50,
52, 54, 56–59, 61
espionage and *CWPS:* 50
Europe and *CWB2:*
324–25; *CWPS:* 9, 30,
43–50, 52–59, 61
France and *CWPS:* 49, 58
Germany and *CWPS:* 48,
50
Great Britain and *CWPS:*
48, 58
Greece and *CWPS:* 58
Harriman, W. Averell, and
CWB1: 172
Iceland and *CWPS:* 58
Italy and *CWPS:* 49, 58
Kennan, George F., and
CWPS: 43
Marshall, George C., and
CWB1: 4, 113; *CWB2:*

324–25; *CWPS:* 33, 43–50

military and *CWB1:* 113; *CWPS:* 54

Molotov, Vyacheslav M., and *CWPS:* 48

"Novikov Telegram" and *CWPS:* 30

peace and *CWPS:* 54–57, 68, 108

Poland and *CWPS:* 48

Soviet Union and *CWB2:* 272, 325; *CWPS:* 30, 44, 45, 48, 57, 61

Stalin, Joseph, and *CWPS:* 30, 48

Truman, Harry S., and *CWB2:* 459; *CWPS:* 33, 52–59

U.S. Congress and *CWPS:* 33, 52–59

Martí, José *CWB1:* 84

Martin, Arthur *CWA1:* 144

Marx, Karl *CWA1:* 6; *CWPS:* 2, 6, 64. *See also* Marxism

Allende, Salvador, and *CWB1:* 18

communism and *CWB2:* 312, 346, 445, 464

Ho Chi Minh and *CWB1:* 181

Marxism *CWA1:* 6; *CWB2:* 228–29, 312, 314–15, 346; *CWPS:* 2, 6

Masters of Deceit CWA1: 108; *CWB1:* 192; *CWPS:* 133

May Fourth Movement *CWB2:* 314, 464

Mazowiecki, Tadeusz *CWA2:* 358

McCarthy Committee *CWA1:* 118; *CWB2:* 334–35; *CWPS:* 171–72

McCarthy, Joseph R. *CWA1:* 117 (ill.), 119 (ill.); CWB2: 329 (ill.), **329–36**, 335 (ill.); *CWPS:* 164 (ill.), 167 (ill.), 169 (ill.), 172 (ill.)

Acheson, Dean G., and *CWB1:* 6; *CWB2:* 334; *CWPS:* 171

censure of *CWA1:* 118, 172; *CWB2:* 220, 335; *CWPS:* 172

Central Intelligence Agency (CIA) and *CWA1:* 118

character of *CWB2:* 331; *CWPS:* 167–68, 172–73

civil rights and *CWB2:* 336

Cohn, Roy, and *CWB2:* 334

communism and *CWB2:* 329, 331

death of *CWA1:* 118; *CWB2:* 335

diplomacy and *CWPS:* 173

early life of *CWB2:* 329–30

Eisenhower, Dwight D., and *CWA1:* 118; *CWB1:* 140; *CWB2:* 334; *CWPS:* 111, 171–72

elections of *CWA1:* 116, 118; *CWB2:* 331, 334; *CWPS:* 166, 171

House Un-American Activities Committee (HUAC) and *CWA1:* 44, 117; *CWB2:* 333

Kennedy, John F., and *CWB2:* 220

La Follette, Robert M., Jr., and *CWB2:* 331

MacArthur, Douglas, and *CWB2:* 299–300

Marshall, George C., and *CWA1:* 44, 117; *CWB2:* 324, 333–34; *CWPS:* 171

McCarthyism and *CWB2:* 332–33; *CWPS:* 166

peace and *CWPS:* 168

Permanent Subcommittee on Investigations and *CWB2:* 334–35

Red Scare and *CWA1:* 43–44, 101, 106, 116–19, 171–72; *CWB2:* 329, 331–36, 376;

CWPS: 110, 124, 163, 166–73

"Speech on Communists in the U.S. State Department Made Before the Women's Republican Club in Wheeling, West Virginia, February 1950" *CWPS:* 166–73

Truman, Harry S., and *CWA1:* 117; *CWB1:* 140; *CWB2:* 299–300, 334, 460, 461; *CWPS:* 171

U.S. Army and *CWB1:* 140; *CWB2:* 334–35; *CWPS:* 172

U.S. State Department and *CWB1:* 6; *CWB2:* 331–32, 334; *CWPS:* 69, 73, 123, 166–71

Voice of America and *CWB2:* 334

Welch, Joseph N., and *CWB2:* 329, 335; *CWPS:* 111, 172

Wiley, Alexander, and *CWB2:* 330–31

World War II and *CWB2:* 330

McCarthyism *CWA1:* 44, 99–100, 101, 116–20, 172; *CWB2:* 332–33; *CWPS:* 166. *See also* Red Scare

McCloy, John J. *CWA1:* 22; *CWPS:* 214, 217, 219–20, 221

McCone, John *CWB1:* 199 (ill.); *CWPS:* 238

McCord, James W., Jr. *CWA2:* 310

McCormick, Robert *CWA1:* 106

McDonald, County Joe *CWA2:* 288, 288 (ill.)

McDowell, John *CWPS:* 138

McFarlane, Robert *CWA2:* 332–33

McGovern, George *CWB2:* 362

McMahon Act *CWB1:* 108

McNamara, Robert S.
  CWA2: 222, 253, 272
    (ill.), 273; *CWB1:* 199
    (ill.); *CWB2:* 337 (ill.),
    337–44, 340 (ill.);
    CWPS: 212, 241, 242,
    258, 259
McNeil, Hector *CWA1:* 143
Media
  espionage and *CWA1:* 143
  Federal Bureau of Investi-
    gation (FBI) and *CWA1:*
    108
  Hoover, J. Edgar, and
    CWA1: 108
  human rights and *CWA2:*
    323
  Red Scare and *CWA1:*
    100, 108, 110, 118
*The Medical-Social Reality in
  Chile CWB1:* 19
Medicare *CWA2:* 282
*The Memoirs of Richard Nixon
  CWB2:* 364
Mensheviks *CWB2:* 427
Message carriers *CWA1:* 136
Middle East *CWA2:* 366
  (ill.); *CWB2:* 363. *See
  also* specific countries
  Camp David Accords and
    CWA2: 328–30
  colonialism and *CWA2:*
    202
  composition of *CWA2:*
    201
  containment and *CWA2:*
    202
  Eisenhower Doctrine and
    CWA2: 192, 203–5
  Great Britain and *CWA2:*
    202
  nation building and
    CWA1: 178–79; *CWA2:*
    202–5
  oil and *CWA2:* 201–2, 205
  Reagan, Ronald, and
    CWA2: 341–42
  Soviet Union and *CWA2:*
    204–5
Military industrial complex
  CWPS: 191

Military Intelligence, Department 5 *CWA1:* 127,
  131, 142
Military Intelligence, Department 6
  definition of *CWA1:* 127
  espionage and *CWA1:*
    136–37, 142, 143,
    145–46, 152
  function of *CWA1:* 131
Military. *See also* Disarmament; U.S. Army; spe-
  cific branches
  Acheson, Dean G., and
    CWB1: 1, 4, 6
  Adenauer, Konrad, and
    CWB1: 9, 12–14
  asymmetrical response
    and *CWA1:* 173–74
  Bevin, Ernest, and *CWB1:*
    35, 38–39
  Brezhnev, Leonid, and
    CWB1: 47, 51
  buildup of *CWB1:* 51;
    CWA1: 144; *CWA2:*
    336; *CWPS:* 102, 104–5,
    186–87, 265
  Bush, George, and *CWB1:*
    54, 58; *CWPS:* 320,
    322–23
  Carter, Jimmy, and
    CWA2: 336
  of China *CWA1:* 52
  Churchill, Winston, and
    CWB1: 101
  Clifford, Clark M., and
    CWB1: 109, 111
  containment and *CWA1:*
    36, 44–45, 48–49, 50;
    CWB2: 213; *CWPS:* 9,
    14, 72, 74–78, 119
  Conventional Force Talks
    in Europe and *CWA2:*
    355
  Conventional Forces in
    Europe (CFE) treaty and
    CWA2: 365–66
  Cuban Missile Crisis and
    CWA2: 226–27; *CWPS:*
    241, 248, 253, 261
  defense alliances and
    CWA1: 176

  draft *CWA2:* 284–85, 336;
    CWB1: 76
  economy and *CWA1:*
    173–74; *CWA2:* 275,
    277–78, 290; *CWPS:*
    119–20, 265
  Eisenhower, Dwight D.,
    and *CWB1:* 134,
    135–39; *CWPS:* 119–20,
    191, 202
  espionage and *CWA1:* 131
  Europe and *CWB2:* 262
  Gorbachev, Mikhail
    CWA2: 355–56; *CWB1:*
    57, 58; *CWPS:* 312–13,
    314
  imperialism and *CWPS:*
    25, 26, 28–30
  in Japan *CWB2:* 297
  Kennedy, John F., and
    CWA2: 256; *CWB2:*
    225
  Khrushchev, Nikita, and
    CWB2: 239–40; *CWPS:*
    190–91, 193–94, 202,
    211, 214–15, 221
  Kim Il Sung and *CWB2:*
    247
  Kissinger, Henry, and
    CWB2: 256
  Latin America and *CWA2:*
    263
  Marshall Plan and *CWB1:*
    113; *CWPS:* 54
  North Atlantic Treaty Or-
    ganization (NATO) and
    CWA1: 37–38; *CWA2:*
    365–66
  in North Korea *CWB2:*
    247
  NSC-68 and *CWB1:* 6
  peace and *CWPS:* 107–8
  Reagan, Ronald, and
    CWA2: 338–39; *CWB1:*
    51; *CWB2:* 392, 393;
    CWPS: 265
  Red Scare and *CWA1:*
    115–16
  of Soviet Union *CWA1:*
    50–52; *CWA2:* 355–56;
    CWB1: 47, 51, 58;
    CWB2: 213, 239–40;
    CWPS: 99, 175, 186–87,

190–91, 193–94, 202, 211, 214–15, 221, 265
Stalin, Joseph, and *CWA1:* 50–52; *CWB2:* 431; *CWPS:* 186–87
Truman, Harry S., and *CWPS:* 76–77
U.S. Congress and *CWPS:* 76–77
Warsaw Pact and *CWA2:* 365–66; *CWPS:* 186
in West Berlin *CWA1:* 69–71
of West Germany *CWA1:* 185
Military-industrial complexes *CWA2:* 275, 276, 277–78, 286, 290
MIRVs. *See* Multiple independently targetable reentry vehicles (MIRVs)
Missiles *CWA2:* 223 (ill.), 239 (ill.), 257 (ill.), 307 (ill.); *CWB1:* 155; *CWB2:* 307, 309, 361, 393. *See also* Cuban Missile Crisis
antiballistic missiles *CWA2:* 247, 258, 303; *CWPS:* 287–88
ballistic missiles *CWPS:* 287–88, 302–3
cruise missiles *CWA2:* 330
Cuban Missile Crisis and *CWPS:* 234, 236, 237–38, 244, 246–47, 251
early warning systems and *CWA2:* 239 (ill.), 240
intercontinental ballistic missiles (ICBMs) *CWA2:* 235, 237, 238–39, 239 (ill.), 244, 257 (ill.), 257–58, 303–4, 307 (ill.), 330
multiple independently targetable reentry vehicles (MIRVs) *CWA2:* 303, 304
nuclear weapons and *CWA2:* 196–99, 235–37, 238–39, 244

race for *CWA2:* 196–99
reconnaissance and *CWA2:* 197–98
second-strike strategies and *CWA2:* 257–58
Strategic Defense Initiative (SDI) and *CWA2:* 342, 344, 352, 354
submarines and *CWA2:* 239–40, 244
Mitrokhin, Vasili *CWA1:* 163–64
Mitterand, François *CWA2:* 356; *CWB2:* 272
Moldavia *CWA1:* 7; *CWB1:* 43–44
Moles. *See also* Espionage
Ames, Aldrich *CWA1:* 162
atomic spies and *CWA1:* 136–37
Cambridge Spies and *CWA1:* 140–44
Central Intelligence Agency (CIA) and *CWA1:* 154
definition of *CWA1:* 125–26, 127
detecting *CWA1:* 153–54
Gordievsky, Oleg *CWA1:* 157
Hanssen, Robert Philip *CWA1:* 162–63
human element of *CWA1:* 150
Mitrokhin, Vasili *CWA1:* 163–64
Penkovsky, Oleg *CWA1:* 151–52
Sombolay, Albert *CWA1:* 161
VENONA and *CWA1:* 133–35
Whalen, William Henry *CWA1:* 153
Wu-Tai Chin, Larry *CWA1:* 158–59
Yurchenko, Vitaly *CWA1:* 158
Molotov Cocktail *CWB2:* 350, 350 (ill.)
Molotov Plan *CWA1:* 28, 32–34; *CWPS:* 45

Molotov, Vyacheslav
CWA1: 11, 15, 33; *CWB2:* 345 (ill.), 345–53, 349 (ill.); *CWPS:* 27 (ill.), 45, 48
agriculture and *CWB2:* 348
Berlin blockade and *CWB2:* 352
Bolshevik Revolution and *CWB2:* 346–47
Churchill, Winston, and *CWB2:* 349
communism and *CWB2:* 345
Communist Party and *CWB2:* 347, 353
death of *CWB2:* 353
early life of *CWB2:* 345–47
as foreign minister *CWB2:* 348–52
Germany and *CWB2:* 348–50, 351
Great Britain and *CWB2:* 348–49
Great Terror and *CWB2:* 348, 351, 352
Gromyko, Andrey, and *CWB1:* 160, 162; *CWB2:* 353
Harriman, W. Averell, and *CWB1:* 171
Hitler, Adolf, and *CWB2:* 348
Khrushchev, Nikita, and *CWB2:* 234, 236, 352–53
Lenin, Vladimir I., and *CWB2:* 347
Marxism and *CWB2:* 346
Molotov Cocktail and *CWB2:* 350
nuclear weapons and *CWB2:* 351
Potsdam Conference and *CWB2:* 351
Pravda and *CWB2:* 346–47
retirement of *CWB2:* 353
Roosevelt, Franklin D., and *CWB2:* 348–50

Stalin, Joseph, and *CWB2:* 345, 346, 347–48, 351, 352
Tehran Conference and *CWB2:* 349
Truman, Harry S., and *CWB2:* 350–51
World War II and *CWB2:* 348–50
Yalta Conference and *CWB2:* 349–50
Monarchy *CWA1:* 6; *CWB2:* 345–46, 380
Mondale, Walter *CWA2:* 345; *CWB1:* 74; *CWPS:* 283
Money *CWA1:* 62
Monroe Doctrine *CWA1:* 36, 186–87, 187 (ill.)
Monroe, James *CWA1:* 186–87
Moody, Juanita *CWA2:* 225
Moon *CWA2:* 199
Moorer, Thomas H. *CWB2:* 261 (ill.)
Morality *CWPS:* 171, 284
Mosaddeq, Mohammed *CWA1:* 169, 178
Movies *CWA1:* 100, 108, 110; *CWA2:* 236
Movies *CWB1:* 189, 192
"Mrs. Franklin D. Roosevelt's Address to the Democratic National Convention on the Importance of the United Nations" *CWPS:* 90–98
Mujahedeen *CWA2:* 335, 336, 340
Multiple independently targetable reentry vehicles (MIRVs) *CWA2:* 303, 304
Murrow, Edward R. *CWA1:* 118; *CWB2:* 334
Music *CWA2:* 287–88
Mutual assured destruction (MAD) *CWA2:* 234–35, 236, 305, 342–43, 374; *CWB2:* 260–61
My African Journey CWB1: 102

The Mysterious Valley CWB2: 383
Mzhevandze, Vassily *CWB2:* 417

N

Nagasaki *CWA1:* 17, 18 (ill.), 87–88, 135
deaths in *CWB2:* 458
nuclear weapons and *CWB2:* 285, 297, 371, 372, 409, 432
Truman, Harry S., and *CWB2:* 458
Nagy, Imre *CWA2:* 194, 196
Napalm *CWA2:* 283–84, 284 (ill.)
NASA. *See* National Aeronautics and Space Administration (NASA)
Nasser, Gamal Abdel *CWA2:* 193, 202–3, 204 (ill.), 204–5; *CWB1:* 131; *CWB2:* 306, 450
Nathaniel Branden Institute *CWB2:* 384
Nation building
Africa and *CWA2:* 206–8, 325–27; *CWB2:* 310, 470
Angola and *CWA2:* 308
Brezhnev, Leonid, and *CWA2:* 325–27; *CWB1:* 50
Castro, Fidel, and *CWB1:* 83, 88
Chile and *CWA2:* 308
China and *CWB2:* 470
colonialism and *CWA1:* 176–78
definition of *CWA1:* 168
Eisenhower, Dwight D., and *CWA1:* 177, 178–80
Gromyko, Andrey, and *CWB1:* 164
Iran and *CWA1:* 178–79; *CWA2:* 308
Kennedy, John F., and *CWA1:* 177

Khrushchev, Nikita, and *CWA1:* 177; *CWA2:* 325
Latin America and *CWA1:* 179–80; *CWA2:* 261–65, 339–41
Middle East and *CWA1:* 178–79; *CWA2:* 202–5
Nicaragua and *CWA1:* 180
Paraguay and *CWA1:* 180
Reagan, Ronald, and *CWA2:* 339–41
Soviet Union and *CWA1:* 180; *CWA2:* 202, 203, 254, 307–8, 325–27; *CWB1:* 50, 164
Third World and *CWA1:* 175–82; *CWA2:* 254, 307–8, 325–27; *CWB1:* 50, 83
Zhou Enlai and *CWB2:* 470
National Academy of Sciences *CWA1:* 82–83; *CWB2:* 371
National Aeronautics and Space Administration (NASA) *CWA2:* 197, 198–99; *CWB1:* 142
National Defense Education Act *CWA2:* 197
National Education Association *CWA1:* 115; *CWPS:* 163
National Endowment for Democracy *CWA2:* 339
National Guard *CWB2:* 222
National Popular Liberation Army (ELAS) *CWPS:* 34, 41
National Press Club *CWB1:* 5
National Security Act *CWA1:* 28, 34–35, 130; *CWB1:* 109
National Security Agency (NSA)
Cuban Missile Crisis and *CWA2:* 221, 224
definition of *CWA1:* 127; *CWA2:* 214
espionage and *CWA1:* 131

formation of *CWA1:* 131

Hiss, Alger, and *CWA1:* 114

VENONA and *CWA1:* 132

National Security Council (NSC) *CWPS:* 77 (ill.)

containment and *CWA1:* 28, 32, 44–45; *CWPS:* 62, 72, 74–77

Cuba and *CWPS:* 233–34

Cuban Missile Crisis and *CWA2:* 221–25; *CWPS:* 234, 236

formation of *CWA1:* 28, 34, 130–31; *CWB1:* 109

Iran-Contra scandal and *CWA2:* 332–33

Kirkpatrick, Jeane, and *CWB2:* 251

Kissinger, Henry, and *CWB2:* 257

Marshall, George C., and *CWB2:* 324

NSC-20 *CWA1:* 32; *CWPS:* 53

NSC-30 *CWA1:* 32; *CWPS:* 53

NSC-68 *CWA1:* 28, 44–45, 46, 48, 115–16, 173; *CWB1:* 6; *CWPS:* 62, 69, 71–77, 119

nuclear weapons and *CWPS:* 53

Rice, Condoleezza, and *CWB2:* 404–5

"National Security Council Report on Soviet Intentions (NSC-68)" *CWPS:* 71–78

National Youth Administration (NYA) *CWB1:* 195–96

Nationalism *CWA1:* 17; *CWB2:* 428; *CWPS:* 271. See also Nation building

Nationalists *CWA1:* 38–42, 50; *CWPS:* 61–62, 64–66. See also Nation building

Chiang Kai-shek and *CWB1:* 93–97; *CWB2:* 465, 466, 467

revolution and *CWB1:* 117; *CWB2:* 315–16, 324, 465, 466, 467

Nationalization

by Attlee, Clement R. *CWB1:* 28–29

in Chile *CWB1:* 21, 22, 23; *CWB2:* 263, 362

in Cuba *CWB1:* 86

in Great Britain *CWB1:* 28–29

in Soviet Union *CWB2:* 380–81

of Suez Canal *CWB2:* 306

NATO. See North Atlantic Treaty Organization (NATO)

Nazi-Soviet Non-Aggression Pact *CWA1:* 6–8, 10

Nazi Party *CWB1:* 126

Nazism *CWA1:* 15, 81

The Necessity for Choice CWB2: 256

Nehru, Jawaharlal *CWB2:* 450, 470

Netherlands *CWA1:* 37

New Deal *CWA1:* 103–4; *CWB1:* 64; *CWB2:* 389, 455

New Life Movement *CWB1:* 94

New Look *CWA1:* 173–75, 178; *CWB1:* 129

New Zealand *CWA1:* 50

Newton, Huey *CWA2:* 281

Ngo Dinh Diem *CWA1:* 169, 182; *CWA2:* 253, 269–70, 283; *CWB1:* 129 (ill.)

Nicaragua *CWA1:* 180; *CWA2:* 330–33, 355; *CWB1:* 56, 81; *CWB2:* 398

Nichols, K. D. *CWB2:* 374 (ill.)

Nikita Khrushchev and the Creation of a Superpower CWPS: 175, 199, 250, 256

9/11. See September 11, 2001, terrorist attacks

Ninjas *CWA1:* 141

Nitze, Paul H. *CWA1:* 44–45; *CWB1:* 6; *CWPS:* 62, 69, 71–78, 73 (ill.)

Nixon Center for Peace and Freedom *CWB2:* 365

Nixon Doctrine *CWA2:* 311–12; *CWPS:* 264, 267–73, 276

Nixon, Pat *CWA2:* 301; *CWPS:* 264, 275, 280–81

Nixon, Richard M. *CWA2:* 305 (ill.), 311 (ill.); CWB1: 48 (ill.), 165 (ill.); *CWB2:* 237 (ill.), 261 (ill.), 354 (ill.), 354–65, 357 (ill.), 361 (ill.), 362 (ill.); *CWPS:* 139 (ill.), 196 (ill.), 268 (ill.), 275 (ill.), 277 (ill.)

ABM treaty and *CWB2:* 262

Acheson, Dean G., and *CWB1:* 8

Allende, Salvador, and *CWB1:* 22–23; *CWB2:* 362

Asia and *CWPS:* 264, 267–73, 276

as attorney *CWB2:* 355, 358

as author *CWB2:* 358, 364

Brezhnev, Leonid, and *CWA2:* 273, 304, 307; *CWB1:* 48–49, 50; *CWB2:* 261–62, 360–61; *CWPS:* 264–65, 280

Bush, George, and *CWB1:* 55; *CWB2:* 364

character of *CWB2:* 355

"Checkers Speech" and *CWB2:* 356

Chile and *CWA2:* 308; *CWB1:* 22–23; *CWB2:* 362

China and *CWA2:* 300–302, 311, 312; *CWB1:* 98–99; *CWB2:* 260, 313, 354, 359, 360, 470; *CWPS:* 69, 264, 270, 274–81

Christmas bombing and *CWB2:* 359

civil rights and *CWB2:* 357, 358–59

Clinton, Bill, and *CWB2:* 364

Cold War and *CWB2:* 354

comebacks of *CWB2:* 358, 364

communism and *CWA2:* 251, 311–12; *CWB2:* 354, 355–56; *CWPS:* 280

containment and *CWPS:* 264, 268–73

culture and *CWPS:* 278, 280

death of *CWB2:* 365

détente and *CWA2:* 310, 311, 314; *CWB1:* 48–49; *CWB2:* 354, 360–61; *CWPS:* 264–65

domestic agenda of *CWB2:* 358–59

early life of *CWB2:* 354–55

East Germany and *CWB1:* 14

economy and *CWPS:* 271, 272

Eisenhower, Dwight D., and *CWB1:* 139–40; *CWB2:* 356, 358; *CWPS:* 100–101

elections of *CWA2:* 212, 251, 273, 312; *CWB1:* 197, 204; *CWB2:* 221, 257, 259, 355, 356, 358, 362, 390; *CWPS:* 264

Ford, Gerald, and *CWB1:* 74; *CWB2:* 364

freedom and *CWPS:* 279

Gorton, John Grey, and *CWPS:* 269

Gromyko, Andrey, and *CWB1:* 164–65

Harriman, W. Averell, and *CWB1:* 175

Hiss, Alger, and *CWB2:* 356

House Un-American Activities Committee and *CWB2:* 332–33, 356

imperialism and *CWB2:* 361–62

"Informal Remarks in Guam with Newsmen (Nixon Doctrine), July 25, 1969" *CWPS:* 267–73

Iran and *CWA2:* 308

Khrushchev, Nikita, and *CWB2:* 238, 357; *CWPS:* 195

Kissinger, Henry, and *CWB2:* 257, 259, 261–62, 262–63, 359

"kitchen debate" and *CWB2:* 237 (ill.), 238, 357

Latin America and *CWB2:* 361–62

Mao Zedong and *CWA2:* 301; *CWB2:* 313, 470; *CWPS:* 276

Middle East and *CWB2:* 363

military draft and *CWA2:* 336

Nixon Doctrine and *CWA2:* 311–12; 267–73, 276

North Korea and *CWB2:* 246; *CWPS:* 270

North Vietnam and *CWPS:* 270

nuclear weapons and *CWA2:* 305; *CWB1:* 48–49; *CWB2:* 359, 360–61; *CWPS:* 280

October War and *CWB1:* 50; *CWB2:* 262, 363

Pacific Rim and *CWPS:* 268–69

Pahlavi, Mohammed Reza, and *CWA2:* 308

peace and *CWB2:* 359, 365; *CWPS:* 270–71, 277–78, 279

presidency of *CWB2:* 358–64

Reagan, Ronald, and *CWB2:* 364, 390

Red Scare and *CWA1:* 44, 109, 113, 114; *CWB2:* 332–33

"Remarks at Andrews Air Force Base on Returning from the People's Republic of China, February 28, 1972" *CWPS:* 274–81

Republic of China and *CWB1:* 98–99; *CWB2:* 260, 360, 470

reputation of *CWB2:* 355

resignation of *CWB2:* 264, 363–64; *CWPS:* 264–65

retirement of *CWB2:* 364–65

Russia and *CWB2:* 364–65

Shanghai Communiqué *CWB2:* 360

Silent Majority and *CWA2:* 276, 288–89; *CWB2:* 359

Soviet Union and *CWB1:* 48–49, 164–65; *CWB2:* 261–62, 354, 359, 360–61; *CWPS:* 275, 280

Strategic Arms Limitation Talks (SALT) and *CWA2:* 304; *CWB1:* 164–65; *CWB2:* 261, 360–61; *CWPS:* 280

Taiwan and *CWA2:* 301; *CWB1:* 98–99; *CWPS:* 276, 278

in U.S. Congress *CWB2:* 355–56

vice presidency of *CWB2:* 356–57; *CWPS:* 100–101

Vietnam War and *CWA2:* 276, 288–89, 290, 301, 311, 312–13; *CWB1:* 50, 175; *CWB2:* 257, 259, 359–60, 362–63; *CWPS:* 264, 268, 269, 271–72, 274–76

Vietnamization and *CWB2:* 359

Watergate scandal and *CWA2:* 298, 299, 310; *CWB1:* 55, 74; *CWB2:* 262, 264, 363–64; *CWPS:* 264–65, 282

World War II and *CWB2:* 355

Zhou Enlai and *CWA2:* 301; *CWB2:* 470

Nobel Literature Prize *CWB1:* 101

Nobel Peace Prize *CWA2:* 361; *CWPS:* 317

Begin, Menachem, and *CWB1:* 79

Brandt, Willy, and *CWB1:* 15

Carter, Jimmy, and *CWB1:* 81

Gorbachev, Mikhail, and *CWB1:* 157; *CWB2:* 421

Kissinger, Henry, and *CWB2:* 255, 259–60

Marshall, George C., and *CWB2:* 321, 325

Sadat, Anwar, and *CWB1:* 79

Sakharov, Andrey, and *CWB2:* 408, 412–13

Nonalignment *CWB2:* 444, 449–50

Noriega, Manuel *CWB1:* 59

North American Air Defense Command (NORAD) *CWA2:* 240

North Atlantic Treaty *CWA1:* 38, 39 (ill.)

North Atlantic Treaty Organization (NATO) *CWPS:* 100, 105–6, 120, 211, 212

Acheson, Dean G., and *CWB1:* 4, 6

Adenauer, Konrad, and *CWB1:* 12–14

Attlee, Clement R., and *CWB1:* 31

Bevin, Ernest, and *CWB1:* 38

Bush, George, and *CWA2:* 363–64

China and *CWB2:* 317

Clifford, Clark M., and *CWB1:* 111, 113

composition of *CWA1:* 38, 68, 171

Conference on Security and Cooperation in Europe (CSCE) and *CWA2:* 365–66

containment and *CWA1:* 28, 168; *CWA2:* 348; *CWB1:* 4, 31, 58, 111, 113; *CWB2:* 271, 327, 434, 437

Conventional Force Talks in Europe and *CWA2:* 355

definition of *CWA1:* 28, 168; *CWA2:* 348

disbanding of *CWA1:* 185–86; *CWA2:* 363

Dulles, John Foster, and *CWB1:* 128

Eisenhower, Dwight D., and *CWB1:* 139

formation of *CWA1:* 37–38; *CWB1:* 4, 38, 113, 128, 139; *CWB2:* 271, 434, 437

France and *CWA2:* 203, 306

Germany and *CWA2:* 363–64; *CWB1:* 58; *CWB2:* 274

Gorbachev, Mikhail, and *CWA2:* 363–64

Great Britain and *CWB2:* 441–42

growth of *CWA1:* 50

Kirkpatrick, Jeane, and *CWB2:* 253

Kohl, Helmut, and *CWB2:* 271–72, 273

Marshall, George C., and *CWB2:* 327

military and *CWA1:* 37–38; *CWA2:* 365–66

nuclear weapons and *CWA1:* 174; *CWA2:* 199, 200, 336–37, 356–57, 364, 373; *CWB2:* 273, 438, 440

Russia and *CWA2:* 370

Soviet Union and *CWA1:* 173; *CWA2:* 363–64; *CWB1:* 113; *CWB2:* 317, 441–42

Stalin, Joseph, and *CWB2:* 317

strength of *CWA1:* 185

Thatcher, Margaret, and *CWB2:* 438, 440, 441–42

Tito, Josip Broz, and *CWB2:* 448

Truman, Harry S., and *CWA1:* 37–38; *CWB2:* 459

Warsaw Pact and *CWA1:* 185; *CWA2:* 364; *CWB2:* 274

West Germany and *CWA1:* 68, 173; *CWB1:* 12–14; *CWB2:* 271–72, 273

Yeltsin, Boris, and *CWA2:* 370

Yugoslavia and *CWB2:* 448

North Korea *CWA1:* 45, 46–48, 50 (ill.); *CWA2:* 373; *CWPS:* 79, 270

Carter, Jimmy, and *CWB1:* 81; *CWB2:* 248

China and *CWB2:* 245–46

communism in *CWB2:* 247

economy of *CWB2:* 244–45, 247

elections in *CWB2:* 247

espionage and *CWB1:* 203

formation of *CWB2:* 242–43, 244

government of *CWB2:* 247

isolationism and *CWB2:* 241, 245, 247

Johnson, Lyndon B., and *CWB1:* 203

Korean Workers' Party in *CWB2:* 242, 247

military in *CWB2:* 247

Nixon, Richard M., and *CWB2:* 246

nuclear weapons and *CWB2:* 247–48

society in *CWB2:* 245

South Korea and *CWB2:* 246, 247

Soviet Union and *CWB2:* 242, 243, 245–46

terrorism and *CWB2:* 246

Third World and *CWB2:* 246

United Nations and *CWB2:* 247

North Vietnam *CWB2:* 257; *CWPS:* 270. *See also* Vietnam

North, Oliver *CWA2:* 332–33; *CWB2:* 398

Novikov, Nikolai V. *CWA1:* 22; *CWPS:* 4, 25–31, 27 (ill.)

"Novikov Telegram" *CWPS:* 4, 25–31

NSA. *See* National Security Agency (NSA)

NSC. *See* National Security Council (NSC)

NSC-68 *CWPS:* 62, 69, **71–78,** 119

Nuclear and Space Arms Talks (NST) *CWA2:* 345

Nuclear energy *CWA2:* 241; *CWPS:* 23, 89, 107, 113–21; *See also* Energy; Nuclear weapons

Acheson, Dean G., and *CWB1:* 3

Baruch, Bernard, and *CWB2:* 373

Germany and *CWB2:* 284–85

Great Britain and *CWB2:* 284, 291

International Atomic Energy Agency and *CWB2:* 352–53

international control of *CWB2:* 373

Kurchatov, Igor, and *CWB2:* 283, 284–85, 289–91, 373

Oppenheimer, J. Robert, and *CWB2:* 213–14, 283, 366, 373

Soviet Union *CWB2:* 289–91

United Nations and *CWB1:* 3; *CWB2:* 373

Nuclear Nonproliferation Treaty *CWA2:* 248, 258; *CWB2:* 248, 281

Nuclear war *CWB2:* 227, 238, 394. *See also* War; World War III

Adenauer, Konrad, and *CWPS:* 220

Berlin and *CWPS:* 209, 210

Civil Defense and *CWPS:* 212–13

Cuban Missile Crisis and *CWPS:* 235, 238, 247, 253, 256, 259, 260, 261

Dulles, John Foster, and *CWPS:* 119

Eisenhower, Dwight D., and *CWPS:* 116–17, 192

Germany and *CWPS:* 220

Kennedy, John F., and *CWPS:* 212–13, 214

Khrushchev, Nikita, and *CWPS:* 192, 198–99, 214, 218, 220

Khrushchev, Sergei, on *CWPS:* 186, 192–93

U.S. Congress and *CWPS:* 212–13

Nuclear weapons *CWA1:* 18 (ill.), 82 (ill.), 86 (ill.), 91 (ill.), 96 (ill.); *CWA2:* 243 (ill.), 307 (ill.). *See also* Atomic bombs; Hydrogen bombs; Manhattan Project; Missiles; Nuclear energy; Weapons

ABM treaty *CWB2:* 262; *CWPS:* 287

accidents and *CWA2:* 242–43

Acheson, Dean G., and *CWB1:* 3, 6

Adenauer, Konrad, and *CWA1:* 171

asymmetrical response and *CWA1:* 173–75

Attlee, Clement R., and *CWB1:* 31

Baker, James, and *CWB2:* 421

balance of *CWA1:* 169; *CWA2:* 374

Beria, Lavrenty, and *CWB2:* 433

Berlin and *CWA1:* 62, 64–65, 70

Bevin, Ernest, and *CWB1:* 31, 38

Brandt, Willy, and *CWB1:* 15

Brezhnev, Leonid, and *CWA2:* 256–58, 304, 305, 323, 330, 336–37; *CWB1:* 47, 48–49, 77–78, 166; *CWB2:* 360–61; *CWPS:* 280

brinkmanship and *CWA1:* 167, 168, 169, 184; *CWB1:* 129

Bush, George, and *CWA2:* 356–57, 362, 368, 369–70, 372; *CWB1:* 57, 58; *CWPS:* 295, 296, 303–4, 311, 320, 322–23

Carter, Jimmy, and *CWA2:* 315, 323, 330, 336, 337; *CWB1:* 49, 70, 74–75, 77–78, 81, 166; *CWB2:* 248, 392

China and *CWA1:* 185; *CWA2:* 206, 246–47, 258, 266, 300, 373; *CWB2:* 318

Churchill, Winston, and *CWA1:* 171; *CWB1:* 31, 108

Cold War and *CWA2:* 233–35; *CWB2:* 366–67; *CWPS:* 192–93

Commonwealth of Independent States (CIS) and *CWA2:* 370

Conference on Security and Cooperation in Europe and *CWB2:* 265

containment and *CWA1:* 32, 92, 93; *CWB2:* 272–73; *CWPS:* 9, 14

control of *CWPS:* 94–95

cost of *CWA2:* 372; *CWPS:* 104–5, 324

countries with *CWA2:* 373

Cuba and *CWA2:* 219–20, 248, 265; *CWB1:* 88–91

Cuban Missile Crisis and *CWB1:* 88–91; *CWPS:* 121, 234, 238, 242–43, 244, 246–47, 248, 256

détente and *CWB1:* 48–49

deterrence and *CWB1:* 108, 140; *CWB2:* 440–41; *CWPS:* 53

deterrent effect of *CWA1:* 169, 175; *CWA2:* 234–35, 256, 374

development of *CWA1:* 9, 80–84, 87, 88–91, 92–95, 135, 171; *CWA2:* 244; *CWB1:* 6, 31, 38, 150; *CWB2:* 212, 283, 285–88, 351, 366, 371–72, 375, 409, 410, 432, 433, 458; *CWPS:* 69, 114, 116

Dulles, John Foster, and *CWA1:* 171; *CWB2:* 256

early warning systems and *CWA2:* 239 (ill.), 240

economy and *CWPS:* 119–20

Eisenhower, Dwight D., and *CWA1:* 70, 170–71; *CWA2:* 200–201; *CWB1:* 140, 144; *CWB2:* 215; *CWPS:* 89, 102, 113–21

espionage and *CWA1:* 9, 14, 19, 43, 88–89, 90–91, 108, 115, 128, 135–40, 143; *CWA2:* 197–98; *CWB1:* 191–92; *CWB2:* 285, 287, 333, 351; *CWPS:* 5, 73, 133

Federal Bureau of Investigation and *CWPS:* 133

Ford, Gerald, and *CWB1:* 166

France and *CWA2:* 247, 373

Germany and *CWA1:* 81–82, 85; *CWA2:*
200–201, 364; *CWB2:* 370, 371

Gorbachev, Mikhail, and *CWA2:* 351, 352–55, 356–57, 364, 368, 369–70, 372; *CWB1:* 56, 58, 154–55; *CWB2:* 395–96, 418; *CWPS:* 265–66, 284–92, 293, 295, 299–300, 302–4, 308, 314, 319

Great Britain and *CWA1:* 138; *CWA2:* 245–46, 373; *CWB1:* 31, 38, 108; *CWB2:* 307, 309, 440–41

Gromyko, Andrey, and *CWB1:* 164–65, 166

Harriman, W. Averell, and *CWB1:* 173

Hitler, Adolf, and *CWA1:* 81–82

hotline for *CWA2:* 230, 241–44; *CWB1:* 91; *CWB2:* 238; *CWPS:* 261

India and *CWA2:* 373

inspections of *CWPS:* 95, 102–3, 108, 188–89, 201

intelligence and *CWA1:* 90, 135

Intermediate-range Nuclear Force (INF) treaty and *CWA2:* 354–55, 372; *CWB2:* 396, 420; *CWPS:* 290, 293, 300, 302–3

Iran and *CWA2:* 373

Iraq and *CWA2:* 373

Johnson, Lyndon B., and *CWA2:* 247, 258; *CWB1:* 204

Kennan, George F., and *CWB2:* 212, 213, 215; *CWPS:* 72

Kennedy, John F., and *CWA2:* 246, 256–58; *CWB2:* 227–28, 341

Khrushchev, Nikita, and *CWA1:* 70, 174–75; *CWA2:* 200–201; *CWB1:* 144; *CWB2:*
226–27, 227–28, 235, 238–39, 411; *CWPS:* 120, 175, 190–91, 220

Kim Il Sung and *CWB2:* 247–48

Kissinger, Henry, and *CWA2:* 305; *CWB2:* 256, 260–62; *CWPS:* 280

Kohl, Helmut, and *CWB2:* 272–73

Korean War and *CWA1:* 47, 48; *CWPS:* 63, 80–81

Kosygin, Aleksey, and *CWA2:* 247

Kurchatov, Igor, and *CWB2:* 285–88, 289–91, 373, 433

Latin America and *CWA2:* 248

Limited Test-Ban Treaty of 1963 *CWB1:* 91, 173; *CWB2:* 227–28, 238–39, 309; *CWPS:* 261

Macmillan, Harold, and *CWB2:* 307, 309

Malenkov, Georgy M., and *CWA1:* 170–71

Manhattan Project and *CWA1:* 9, 13–14, 79–81, 83–86, 87, 88–89, 90–91, 115, 128, 135, 138, 139; *CWA2:* 244

Mao Zedong and *CWA2:* 206

McNamara, Robert S., and *CWB2:* 341

missiles and *CWA2:* 196–99, 235–37, 238–39, 244

Molotov, Vyacheslav, and *CWB2:* 351

mutual assured destruction (MAD) and *CWA2:* 234–35, 236, 305, 342–43, 374; *CWB2:* 260–61

National Academy of Sciences and *CWA1:* 82–83

National Security Council and *CWPS:* 53

negotiations concerning *CWA1:* 19, 95, 170–71, 185, 186–87; *CWA2:* 199–201, 210, 211–12, 230, 244, 247–48, 258, 260–61, 265, 273, 297–98, 302–5, 323, 328, 330, 338, 342, 344–45, 351, 352–55, 356–57, 368; *CWB1:* 48–49, 56, 144, 155, 164–65, 166, 173, 204; *CWB2:* 227–28, 238–39, 252, 261–62, 395–96; *CWPS:* 121, 175, 261, 265–66, 280, 284–92, 293, 320

Nitze, Paul H., and *CWB1:* 6

Nixon, Richard M., and *CWA2:* 305; *CWB1:* 48–49; *CWB2:* 359, 360–61; *CWPS:* 280

North Atlantic Treaty Organization (NATO) and *CWA1:* 174; *CWA2:* 199, 200, 336–37, 356–57, 364, 373; *CWB2:* 273, 438, 440; *CWPS:* 120

North Korea and *CWA2:* 373; *CWB2:* 247–48

Nuclear and Space Arms Talks and *CWA2:* 345

Nuclear Nonproliferation Treaty *CWB2:* 248, 281

October War and *CWA2:* 309–10

Oppenheimer, J. Robert, and *CWB2:* 366, 368, 370–72, 375

opposition to *CWA2:* 243, 244–46

Outer Space Treaty *CWPS:* 283

Pakistan and *CWA2:* 373

peace and *CWPS:* 104–5, 107–8, 109, 113–21

race for *CWA1:* 22, 24, 43, 88–96, 144, 168, 169, 173–75, 185; *CWA2:* 199, 233–38, 244, 246–47, 256–58, 275,

298, 320–21, 336–39, 342–45; *CWB1:* 31, 51, 74–75, 154, 166; *CWB2:* 213, 290, 341, 396, 410, 418, 432; *CWPS:* 26, 89, 113, 114, 115–18, 119–21, 168, 190–91, 192, 199, 201, 282–83, 284

Reagan, Ronald, and *CWA2:* 319, 320–21, 338, 342–45, 352–55, 372; *CWB1:* 56, 78, 155; *CWB2:* 252, 392, 395–96, 418; *CWPS:* 265–66, 284–92, 293, 300, 303

reconnaissance and *CWB2:* 288

Red Scare and *CWB2:* 333

Roosevelt, Eleanor, and *CWPS:* 94–95

Roosevelt, Franklin D., and *CWA1:* 9, 81–82, 83, 94; *CWA2:* 244

Russia and *CWA2:* 370, 373

Sakharov, Andrey, and *CWB2:* 290

second-strike strategies and *CWA2:* 256–58

Shevardnadze, Eduard, and *CWA2:* 355; *CWB2:* 418–20, 421; *CWPS:* 291

Shultz, George, and *CWA2:* 344; *CWB1:* 166; *CWB2:* 418–20; *CWPS:* 300, 303

South Africa and *CWA2:* 373

Soviet Union and *CWA1:* 22, 43, 70, 88–91, 95–96, 115, 135–40, 174–75; *CWA2:* 200–201, 235, 236–37, 240–41, 244–45, 247, 256–58, 303–4, 305, 323, 330, 336–39, 349, 362, 364, 369–70, 372; *CWB1:* 6, 47, 48–49, 50, 56, 58, 70, 77–78, 88–91, 154–55, 164–65,

166, 204; *CWB2:* 213, 226–28, 235, 238–39, 283, 285–88, 289–91, 333, 351, 360–61, 373, 375, 395–96, 409, 410–11, 418, 421, 432, 433, 434, 440–41; *CWPS:* 69, 71, 94–95, 102, 113, 114, 116–17, 120–21, 175, 190–91, 220, 265–66, 280, 284–92, 293, 295, 296, 299–300, 302–4, 308, 314

Stalin, Joseph, and *CWA1:* 9, 14, 88–89; *CWB2:* 285, 351, 432

Strategic Arms Limitation Talks (SALT) and *CWA2:* 248, 297–98, 302–5, 320, 323, 330, 335, 336, 338, 353; *CWB1:* 48, 49, 50, 70, 77–78, 164–65, 166, 204; *CWB2:* 255, 261, 360–61, 390; *CWPS:* 280, 285, 287–92

Strategic Arms Reduction Talks (START) and *CWA2:* 352, 357, 372

Strategic Defense Initiative (SDI) and *CWA2:* 342–45, 352, 354; *CWB2:* 273, 393, 395–96; *CWPS:* 282–83, 285, 287–92, 320, 323

Strategic Triad and *CWA2:* 234, 235, 238–40

strength of *CWA1:* 79, 88, 95; *CWA2:* 219, 240–41; *CWB2:* 409, 411; *CWPS:* 101, 115, 242–43

stockpiles of *CWA1:* 93

test bans and *CWA2:* 199–201, 210, 212, 230, 234, 244, 261; *CWB1:* 173; *CWB2:* 238–39

testing of *CWA1:* 13–14, 43, 79–80, 85–86, 87, 88, 90, 91, 95–96, 115, 135; *CWA2:* 233, 236, 240–41, 244–45, 260;

Organization of American States (OAS) *CWA1:* 36; *CWA2:* 226, 265, 330–31; *CWB1:* 60; *CWB2:* 327, 377; *CWPS:* 241, 248

Organization of Petroleum Exporting Countries (OPEC) *CWB1:* 76; *CWB2:* 363

Organized crime *CWB1:* 185, 189

Orlov, Vadim *CWPS:* 259

Ortega, Daniel *CWA2:* 332, 333 (ill.); *CWB2:* 398

OSRD. *See* Office of Scientific Research and Development (OSRD)

OSS. *See* Office of Strategic Services (OSS)

Ostopolitik CWA2: 305–6; *CWB1:* 15

Oswald, Lee Harvey *CWA2:* 254; *CWB2:* 228–29

"Our First Line of Defense" *CWPS:* 62, 64–70

Outer Space Treaty *CWA2:* 248, 258, 344; *CWPS:* 283

P

Pace, Stephen *CWB1:* 72

Pacific Rim *CWPS:* 268–69

Pahlavi, Mohammed Reza *CWA1:* 178; *CWA2:* 308, 332–34; *CWB1:* 79; *CWB2:* 391

Pakistan *CWA2:* 336, 373; *CWB1:* 29

Palestine *CWA2:* 328–29, 341; *CWB1:* 29, 36–37

Palestine Liberation Organization (PLO) *CWA2:* 328–29; *CWB1:* 50

Palmer, A. Mitchell *CWA1:* 102–3, 103 (ill.); *CWB1:* 187

Palmer Raids *CWA1:* 103; *CWB1:* 187

Palomares Incident *CWA2:* 242, 243, 243 (ill.)

Pan Am bombing *CWA2:* 376; *CWB2:* 399

Panama *CWA2:* 262–63, 264 (ill.); *CWB1:* 59–60, 77, 81

Panama Canal *CWB1:* 59, 77, 125

Paraguay *CWA1:* 180

Partisans *CWB2:* 446

Pasternak, Boris *CWB2:* 234

Paul VI (pope) *CWB1:* 164

Peace *CWA2:* 246 (ill.)
Adenauer, Konrad, and *CWPS:* 110
Asia and *CWPS:* 107, 270–71, 277
Berlin and *CWPS:* 213–14
China and *CWPS:* 277–78, 279
Churchill, Winston, and *CWPS:* 110
Cold War and *CWA2:* 374
counterculture and *CWA2:* 287
Cuban Missile Crisis and *CWPS:* 246–47, 248–49, 256, 258, 260
democracy and *CWPS:* 54–56
Dulles, John Foster, and *CWB1:* 126; *CWPS:* 110
Eastern Bloc and *CWPS:* 107, 108
Eisenhower, Dwight D., and *CWB1:* 134; *CWPS:* 88–89, 99–111, 113–21, 188, 192
Europe and *CWA2:* 364–67
freedom and *CWPS:* 54–55, 57
Gorbachev, Mikhail, and *CWPS:* 294, 298–99, 300–302, 314
Johnson, Lyndon B., and *CWB1:* 200, 204
Kennedy, John F., and *CWB2:* 221; *CWPS:* 213–14, 246–47, 248–49
Khrushchev, Nikita, and *CWB2:* 352; *CWPS:*

175, 187–88, 192, 195–203, 256, 258, 260
Kirkpatrick, Jeane, on *CWB2:* 249
Korean War and *CWPS:* 106–7, 108
Kurchatov, Igor, and *CWB2:* 283, 289–91, 373
Malenkov, Georgy M., and *CWPS:* 99, 101
Marshall Plan and *CWPS:* 54–57, 68, 108
McCarthy, Joseph R., and *CWPS:* 168
military and *CWPS:* 107–8
movements for *CWA2:* 245–46
Nixon, Richard M., and *CWB2:* 359, 365; *CWPS:* 270–71, 277–78, 279
North Atlantic Treaty Organization and *CWPS:* 105–6
nuclear energy and *CWA2:* 241; *CWPS:* 89, 107, 113–21
nuclear weapons and *CWPS:* 104–5, 107–8, 109, 113–21
Oppenheimer, J. Robert, and *CWB2:* 213–14, 283, 373
Reagan, Ronald, and *CWPS:* 284–85
Roosevelt, Franklin D., and *CWPS:* 91, 92
Soviet Union and *CWPS:* 53–54, 55–56, 99, 101–2, 103–10, 213–14, 294, 298–99, 300–302, 314
strength and *CWPS:* 189
symbol for *CWA2:* 245, 246
Truman, Harry S., and *CWPS:* 38, 53–54, 54–56, 57
United Nations and *CWPS:* 21, 22, 38, 56,

88, 90–98, 103, 108, 300–302

Vietnam War and *CWA2:* 271–73, 312–13; *CWB1:* 175, 204; *CWPS:* 272

war and *CWPS:* 83–84

weapons and *CWPS:* 104–5, 107–8, 109

World War II and *CWA2:* 364; *CWB1:* 106; *CWPS:* 53–54, 55–56

"Peace and Progress Must Triumph in Our Time" *CWPS:* 175, **195–203**

Peace Corps *CWA2:* 252, 255; *CWB2:* 221

"Peaceful Uses of Atomic Energy" *CWPS:* 89, **113–21**

Pearce, Robert *CWB1:* 25

Pearl Harbor *CWA1:* 8, 104–5; *CWB1:* 105, 135–36; *CWB2:* 296, 370–71

Pelton, Ronald *CWA1:* 158

Pendergast, Thomas *CWB2:* 454

Penkovsky, Oleg *CWA1:* 151–52, 152 (ill.)

People's Republic of China (PRC) *CWA1:* 41–42; *CWB1:* 96–97, 117; *CWB2:* 243, 467; *CWPS:* 66. *See also* China; Republic of China (ROC); Taiwan

Perestroika *CWA2:* 348, 351, 358, 361; *CWPS:* 300–301, 302, 309, 312–13

adoption of *CWB1:* 56

China and *CWB1:* 121

Gorbachev, Mikhail, and *CWB1:* 146, 153; *CWB2:* 395, 414, 416, 418

Shevardnadze, Eduard, and *CWB2:* 416

Permanent Subcommittee on Investigations *CWB2:* 334–35. *See also* McCarthy Committee

Pershing, John J. *CWB2:* 322

Persian Gulf War *CWA1:* 161; *CWB1:* 60; *CWB2:* 421; *CWPS:* 317, 324

Peterson, J. W. *CWPS:* 259

Phan Boi Chau *CWB1:* 177

Philby, Kim *CWA1:* 128, 140–41, 142, 143, 144; *CWPS:* 50

Philippines *CWB2:* 295, 296–97, 302

Photography *CWA1:* 137 (ill.)

Cuban Missile Crisis and *CWA2:* 222, 225

espionage and *CWA1:* 136, 137 (ill.), 147–50; *CWA2:* 198, 222

Pinay, Antoine *CWA1:* 175 (ill.)

Ping-pong *CWA2:* 301, 302

Pinochet Ugarte, Augusto *CWA2:* 308; *CWB2:* 263, 362

Pius XII (pope) *CWPS:* 49

PLO. *See* Palestine Liberation Organization (PLO)

Podgorny, Nikolay *CWB1:* 46

Poetry *CWA2:* 292, 293

Poindexter, John *CWA2:* 332–33; *CWB2:* 398

Poland *CWA2:* 194 (ill.); *CWPS:* 20, 48

boundary of *CWB1:* 66

Brandt, Willy, and *CWB1:* 15

Brezhnev, Leonid, and *CWB1:* 51

communism in *CWA1:* 57; *CWB1:* 36–37

Communist Party in *CWA1:* 11, 12–13; *CWA2:* 357–58

democracy and *CWA2:* 357–58; *CWB2:* 421

elections in *CWA2:* 357–58; *CWB1:* 36–37, 66, 171; *CWB2:* 431

freedom in *CWA2:* 193–94

Germany and *CWB2:* 431

Gorbachev, Mikhail, and *CWA2:* 358

Gromyko, Andrey, and *CWB1:* 166

Khrushchev, Nikita, and *CWA2:* 193–94

labor in *CWA2:* 193–94, 357–58

Ostopolitik and *CWA2:* 306

riots in *CWA2:* 193–94

Solidarity in *CWB2:* 394

Soviet Union and *CWA1:* 9, 10, 11, 12–13, 57; *CWA2:* 358; *CWB1:* 36–37, 51, 66, 161, 166, 171; *CWB2:* 394, 431

Stalin, Joseph, and *CWA1:* 9, 11; *CWB1:* 66

West Germany and *CWB1:* 15

World War II and *CWA1:* 7, 9–10, 11; *CWB1:* 106, 161, 171; *CWB2:* 431

Policy Planning Staff (PPS) *CWB2:* 212

Politburo *CWPS:* 11, 174, 283. *See also* Presidium

in Communist Party *CWB1:* 162–63

Deng Xiaoping and *CWB1:* 118

Gorbachev, Mikhail, and *CWB1:* 152; *CWB2:* 418

Gromyko, Andrey, and *CWB1:* 165

Khrushchev, Nikita, and *CWB2:* 232, 234, 240

Kosygin, Aleksey, and *CWB2:* 279, 280

Molotov, Vyacheslav, and *CWB2:* 347, 352

Zhou Enlai and *CWB2:* 465–66

Political Woman CWB2: 250

Politics *CWA1:* 36; *CWB2:* 213; *CWPS:* 9, 14, 192

Pollard, Jonathan Jay *CWA1:* 159–60

Popular Revolutionary Action Front (FRAP) *CWB1:* 19

Popular Unity Coalition *CWB1:* 17, 20

Portugal *CWA2:* 206

Potsdam Conference *CWA1:* 13–17, 14 (ill.), 16 (ill.), 86, 143; *CWPS:* 22 (ill.)
Attlee, Clement R., and *CWB1:* 28, 35–36, 66; *CWB2:* 431
Bevin, Ernest, and *CWB1:* 35–37
Big Three and *CWB1:* 65, 66
Byrnes, James F., and *CWB1:* 65, 66
Churchill, Winston, and *CWB1:* 35–37
Gromyko, Andrey, and *CWB1:* 161
Molotov, Vyacheslav, and *CWB2:* 351
overview of *CWB1:* 106
Stalin, Joseph, and *CWB1:* 66; *CWB2:* 431
Truman, Harry S., and *CWB1:* 65, 66; *CWB2:* 457

Potsdam Declaration *CWA1:* 17

Poverty *CWB1:* 195, 197–98, 201–3

Powell, Colin *CWB2:* 406 (ill.)

Power *CWPS:* 19, 320

Power, Thomas *CWA2:* 240

Powers, Francis Gary *CWA1:* 149–50; *CWA2:* 211, 240

PPS. *See* Policy Planning Staff (PPS)

Prague Spring *CWA2:* 252, 267–68

Pravda CWB2: 346–47, 427; *CWPS:* 250 (ill.)

PRC. *See* People's Republic of China (PRC)

A Precocious Autobiography CWA2: 293

Present at the Creation: My Years in the State Department CWB1: 8

Presidential Medal of Freedom *CWB1:* 109; *CWB2:* 217, 249, 253, 343

Presidium *CWB1:* 44, 163; *CWB2:* 419. *See also* Politburo

Press *CWPS:* 23–24, 29, 232, 261, 276, 299

Prevention of Nuclear War *CWA2:* 307

Profumo, John *CWB2:* 310

Prohibition Era *CWB1:* 185

Project Apollo *CWA2:* 199

Project Vanguard *CWA2:* 198

Project Y *CWA1:* 83–84

Propaganda *CWB1:* 42, 45, 150, 159, 190
Berlin airlift and *CWA1:* 66
communism and *CWPS:* 135–36, 137–38, 141, 146–65
Federal Bureau of Investigation (FBI) and *CWA1:* 108
Hoover, J. Edgar, and *CWPS:* 126, 127–32
House Un-American Activities Committee and *CWPS:* 137, 146–65
human rights and *CWA2:* 323
Kennan, George F., and *CWPS:* 10
Khrushchev, Nikita, and *CWPS:* 203
"Long Telegram" on *CWPS:* 10
racism and *CWA2:* 282–83
Rand, Ayn, on *CWPS:* 137, 138
Sputnik I and *CWA2:* 196
as weapon *CWA1:* 2, 28, 56, 80, 100, 126, 127, 168; *CWA2:* 192, 234, 252, 276, 298, 320, 348

Property *CWPS:* 1–2, 150, 204
capitalism and *CWA1:* 4, 27, 28, 56, 58, 101, 126, 128, 168, 169; *CWA2:* 192, 214, 216, 298, 299, 320, 348; *CWB1:* 3, 42, 86, 111, 150, 178; *CWB2:* 211, 237, 251–52, 313, 385, 404
collectivism and *CWB2:* 409
communism and *CWA1:* 2, 3, 7, 27–29, 56, 57, 80, 99, 100, 104, 126, 128, 167, 168; *CWA2:* 192, 214, 215, 234, 251, 252, 276, 298, 299, 319–20, 347, 348; *CWB1:* 3, 18, 26, 42, 82, 100, 110, 127, 150, 160, 168, 178, 186; *CWB2:* 211, 223, 231, 278, 295, 312, 331, 340, 346, 366, 385, 389, 404, 410, 426, 445, 458, 464
democracy and *CWB2:* 426
Marxism and *CWA1:* 6

Pulitzer Prize *CWB1:* 8

Purple Heart *CWB2:* 219

Putin, Vladimir *CWA2:* 373; *CWB2:* 419

Q

Quarantine *CWA2:* 214, 225–26, 227–29, 260; *CWB1:* 90; *CWB2:* 227, 238; *CWPS:* 242. *See also* Blockades

Quayle, Dan *CWPS:* 322 (ill.)

R

Rabi, I. I. *CWB2:* 375

Racism *CWA2:* 275–76, 278–83, 279 (ill.), 285; *CWB1:* 63, 68; *CWPS:*

152. *See also* Discrimination; Ethnic conflict; Segregation

Kissinger, Henry, and *CWB2:* 266, 390

Kohl, Helmut, and *CWB2:* 272

Korean Airlines tragedy and *CWA2:* 343; *CWB2:* 394

Latin America and *CWA2:* 339–41

Libya and *CWB2:* 398–99

Middle East and *CWA2:* 341–42

military and *CWA2:* 338–39; *CWB1:* 51; *CWB2:* 392, 393; *CWPS:* 265

nation building and *CWA2:* 339–41

National Endowment for Democracy and *CWA2:* 339

Nicaragua and *CWA2:* 332–33, 355; *CWB2:* 398

Nixon, Richard M., and *CWB2:* 364, 390

Nuclear and Space Arms Talks and *CWA2:* 345

nuclear war and *CWB2:* 394

nuclear weapons and *CWB1:* 56, 78, 155; *CWB2:* 252, 392, 395–96, 418; *CWA2:* 319, 320–21, 338, 342–45, 352–55, 372; *CWPS:* 265–66, 284–92, 293, 300, 303

Ortega, Daniel, and *CWA2:* 332

peace and *CWPS:* 284–85

as radio broadcaster *CWB2:* 388

Reagan Doctrine and *CWA2:* 339; *CWB2:* 397–98

Reaganomics and *CWB2:* 392

Red Scare and *CWA2:* 338; *CWB2:* 389

religion and *CWPS:* 284–85

retirement of *CWB2:* 399

Screen Actors Guild and *CWB2:* 388–89

Shultz, George, and *CWPS:* 283

Soviet Union and *CWA2:* 342; *CWB1:* 56, 155–56, 166, 175; *CWB2:* 216, 252, 392–93, 395–96; *CWPS:* 282–92, 293–94, 295, 312

Strategic Arms Limitation Talks (SALT) and *CWA2:* 338, 353; *CWB1:* 78; *CWB2:* 390, 392

Strategic Arms Reduction Talks (START) and *CWA2:* 352

Strategic Defense Initiative (SDI) and *CWA2:* 342–45, 352, 354; *CWB1:* 155; *CWB2:* 273, 393, 395–96; *CWPS:* 282–83, 285, 287–92

Thatcher, Margaret, and *CWB2:* 441–42

Third World and *CWB2:* 397–99

Truman, Harry S., and *CWB2:* 389

United Nations and *CWA2:* 341, 345; *CWB2:* 395

Vietnam War and *CWB2:* 390

World War II and *CWB2:* 388

Reaganomics *CWB2:* 392

Reconnaissance *CWA1:* 147 (ill.), 148 (ill.), 149 (ill.); *CWB1:* 90; *CWB2:* 227, 288; *CWPS:* 236, 246, 247, 255. *See also* Espionage; Intelligence

Bay of Pigs and *CWA1:* 150

Central Intelligence Agency (CIA) and *CWA1:* 147, 150

Cuban Missile Crisis and *CWA1:* 150; *CWA2:* 222, 223 (ill.), 225

definition of *CWA1:* 127

Eisenhower, Dwight D., and *CWA1:* 148, 150; *CWA2:* 211–12

espionage and *CWA1:* 147–50

Khrushchev, Nikita, and *CWA1:* 150

missiles and *CWA2:* 197–98

satellites and *CWA1:* 150

U-2 aircraft and *CWA1:* 147–50; *CWA2:* 211, 240

Red Army *CWB2:* 316, 466

Red Guard *CWA2:* 266, 267 (ill.), 294, 295, 295 (ill.); *CWB2:* 318, 472

Red Scare. *See also* Mc-Carthyism

African Americans and *CWA1:* 115

Berlin airlift and *CWA1:* 111

blacklisting and *CWB2:* 384, 389

Bolshevik Revolution and *CWA1:* 101–3

Central Intelligence Agency (CIA) and *CWA1:* 118

China and *CWA1:* 111; *CWB2:* 333

civil rights and *CWA1:* 110, 113, 115, 172; *CWB2:* 333

Cold War and *CWA1:* 114

communism and *CWB2:* 332–33, 376, 389

costs of *CWA2:* 372

definition of *CWA1:* 100

democracy and *CWA1:* 108–9

Democratic Party and *CWA1:* 106–7

elections and *CWA1:* 106

espionage and *CWA1:* 44, 107, 112, 113–14

fear and *CWA1:* 11, 105; *CWPS:* 123

Federal Bureau of Investigation (FBI) and *CWA1:* 100, 107, 108; *CWB1:* 189–92

Eisenhower, Dwight D., and *CWB1:* 139

House Un-American Activities Committee and *CWB1:* 191

isolationism and *CWB1:* 170

Kirkpatrick, Jeane, and *CWB2:* 253

Watergate scandal and *CWB2:* 363

Reserve Officers' Training Corps (ROTC) *CWA2:* 285

Reuter, Ernst *CWA1:* 63

Ribbentrop, Joachim von *CWB2:* 348

Ribbentrop-Molotov Pact. *See* Soviet-German Nonaggression Treaty

Rice, Condoleezza *CWB2:* 401 (ill.), **401–7**

Rickover, Hyman G. *CWB1:* 72–73

Rio Pact *CWA1:* 36; *CWB2:* 327, 459

RNC. *See* Republican National Committee (RNC)

Robertson, David *CWB1:* 62

Robinson, Jackie *CWA1:* 115; *CWPS:* 163

ROC. *See* Republic of China (ROC)

Roca, Blas *CWB2:* 239 (ill.)

Rockefeller, Nelson A. *CWB1:* 55, 173; *CWB2:* 256; *CWPS:* 188

Rogers, William P. *CWB2:* 261 (ill.); *CWPS:* 277 (ill.)

Romania *CWA1:* 18; *CWA2:* 360; *CWB1:* 43

Ronald Reagan Washington National Airport *CWB1:* 37

Roosevelt, Eleanor *CWA2:* 315; *CWB1:* 170; *CWPS:* 88, **90–98**, 92 (ill.), 93 (ill.), 95 (ill.), 96 (ill.)

Roosevelt, Franklin D. *CWA1:* 30 (ill.); *CWB1:* 190 (ill.); *CWPS:* 19 (ill.)

Acheson, Dean G., and *CWB1:* 2

Big Three and *CWA1:* 2, 9–10, 29

Bullitt, William C., and *CWB2:* 209

Byrnes, James F., and *CWB1:* 62, 63–64, 64–65

character of *CWA1:* 25

Churchill, Winston, and *CWB1:* 105–6; *CWB2:* 431

Civilian Conservation Corps and *CWB2:* 295

communism and *CWB1:* 185–86, 189; *CWPS:* 125

Davies, Joseph, and *CWB2:* 209–10

death of *CWA1:* 10, 86; *CWB1:* 3, 65, 66, 106, 127, 171; *CWB2:* 350, 452, 457

economy and *CWA1:* 5, 12–13, 103–4

Einstein, Albert, and *CWA2:* 244

Eisenhower, Dwight D., and *CWB1:* 136; *CWPS:* 100

election of *CWB1:* 2, 64, 170; *CWB2:* 456

espionage and *CWA1:* 140, 142

facism and *CWB1:* 185–86, 189

Great Depression and *CWA1:* 5, 103–4; *CWB1:* 64; *CWB2:* 295, 389

Harriman, W. Averell, and *CWB1:* 170–71

health of *CWPS:* 97–98

Hiss, Alger, and *CWB2:* 356

Hoover, J. Edgar, and *CWA1:* 108; *CWB1:* 189; *CWPS:* 125

isolationism and *CWA1:* 6, 12

Japan and *CWB2:* 432

Kennan, George F., and *CWB2:* 209–10

Latin America and *CWA2:* 265

MacArthur, Douglas, and *CWB2:* 296–97

Marshall, George C., and *CWB2:* 323

Molotov, Vyacheslav, and *CWB2:* 348–50

New Deal of *CWB1:* 64; *CWB2:* 389, 455

nuclear weapons and *CWA1:* 9, 81–82, 83, 94; *CWA2:* 244

peace and *CWPS:* 91, 92

Red Scare and *CWA1:* 108

Roosevelt, Eleanor, and *CWPS:* 97–98

Soviet Union and *CWA1:* 5; *CWB2:* 209

Stalin, Joseph, and *CWB1:* 105–6; *CWB2:* 430, 431–32

Tehran Conference and *CWB2:* 431

Truman, Harry S., and *CWB1:* 65; *CWB2:* 455, 456

United Nations and *CWA1:* 12

World War II and *CWB1:* 105–6, 136, 170–71, 196; *CWB2:* 348–50; *CWPS:* 92, 100

Yalta agreements and *CWA1:* 2, 10, 105

Yalta Conference and *CWB1:* 65, 66; *CWB2:* 431, 432; *CWPS:* 18

Roosevelt, Theodore *CWA1:* 187 (ill.)

Rosario Casas, Maria del *CWA1:* 162

Rosenbaum, Alissa Zinovievna. *See* Rand, Ayn

Rosenberg, Ethel *CWA1:* 91, 108, 139 (ill.), 139–40; *CWB1:* 192; *CWPS:* 133

Rosenberg, Julius *CWA1:* 91, 108, 139 (ill.), 139–40; *CWB1:* 192; *CWPS:* 133

ROTC. *See* Reserve Officers' Training Corps (ROTC)

Royal Air Force *CWA1:* 62–66

Royal, Denise *CWB2:* 371–72

Ruby, Jack *CWB2:* 228

Rusk, Dean *CWA2:* 222, 228, 253, 258; *CWB1:* 7 (ill.), 199 (ill.), 201, 202; *CWPS:* 250

Russell, Bertrand *CWA2:* 245

Russia *CWA2:* 371 (ill.), 374 (ill.); *CWPS:* 2, 250 (ill.), 323, 324. *See also* Commonwealth of Independent States (CIS); Russian Federation; Soviet Union

Bolshevik Revolution and *CWA1:* 2, 3–5, 6–7, 100–101, 132

capitalism and *CWA2:* 373

Chechnya and *CWA2:* 375

Communist Party in *CWA1:* 3, 101; *CWA2:* 369, 373

democracy and *CWA2:* 373

economy of *CWA2:* 373

elections in *CWA2:* 373

greatness of *CWA1:* 1

monarchy in *CWA1:* 6

Monroe Doctrine and *CWA1:* 186–87

North Atlantic Treaty Organization (NATO) and *CWA2:* 370

nuclear weapons and *CWA2:* 370, 373

World War I and *CWA1:* 6

Russian Federation *CWA2:* 370, 375

Russian Foreign Intelligence Service (SVR) *CWA1:* 132, 160

Russian Research Centre Kurchatov Institute *CWB2:* 286, 286 (ill.)

Russian Revolution of 1917. *See* Bolshevik Revolution

Ruz Gonzalez, Lina *CWB1:* 83

S

SAC. *See* Strategic Air Command (SAC)

Sadat, Anwar *CWA2:* 329, 329 (ill.); *CWB1:* 78 (ill.), 79

Sakharov, Andrey *CWA2:* 245 (ill.); *CWB1:* 75, 155; *CWB2:* 290, 375, 408 (ill.), **408–15**

Carter, Jimmy, and *CWA2:* 315, 324

exile of *CWA2:* 349, 351

hydrogen bombs and *CWA1:* 95; *CWA2:* 233, 244–45

SALT. *See* Strategic Arms Limitation Talks (SALT)

Sandinista National Liberation Front *CWA2:* 330–32

Satellites *CWA1:* 150, 154–55; *CWA2:* 196, 198, 275

Schlesinger, Arthur M., Jr. *CWPS:* 258

Schlesinger, James *CWB2:* 262

Schmidt, Helmut *CWB2:* 271

School *CWPS:* 149–50, 151, 163. *See also* Education

Schorr, Daniel *CWPS:* 225, 225 (ill.)

Schuman Plan *CWB1:* 12

Scowcroft, Brent *CWB2:* 404–5; *CWPS:* 312

Screen Actors Guild *CWA2:* 338; *CWB2:* 388–89; *CWPS:* 124, 132, 136, 139–41

SDI. *See* Strategic Defense Initiative (SDI)

Seaborg, Glenn T. *CWA1:* 87; *CWB2:* 374 (ill.)

Seale, Bobby *CWA2:* 281

SEATO. *See* Southeast Asia Treaty Organization (SEATO)

Second-strike strategies *CWA2:* 256–58

Secret Intelligence Service (SIS) *CWA1:* 131

Segregation *CWA2:* 278–79, 279 (ill.), 281. *See also* Discrimination; Racism

African Americans and *CWB1:* 68, 71, 73; *CWB2:* 221–22

Byrnes, James F., and *CWB1:* 68

Carter, Jimmy, and *CWB1:* 73

Carter, Lillian Gordy, and *CWB1:* 71

Civil Rights Act of 1964 and *CWB1:* 197

Kennedy, John F., and *CWB2:* 221–22

Rice, Condoleezza *CWB2:* 402–3

Sellers, Peter *CWA2:* 236, 236 (ill.)

Separatism *CWA2:* 281

September 11, 2001, terrorist attacks *CWA2:* 376; *CWB2:* 407; *CWPS:* 324, 325

Serber, Robert *CWA1:* 84

Shadows *CWA1:* 141

Shah of Iran. *See* Pahlavi, Mohammed Reza

Shanghai Communiqué *CWB2:* 360

Shepard, Alan B., Jr. *CWA2:* 198

Shevardnadze, Eduard *CWA2:* 349, 351, 355, 367; *CWB2:* 416 (ill.), **416–24**; *CWPS:* 291, 305

Afghanistan and *CWB2:* 420

Andropov, Yuri, and
CWB2: 417
as author *CWB2:* 423
Baker, James, and *CWB1:*
57; *CWB2:* 420–21
Cold War and *CWB2:* 416
Commonwealth of Independent States and
CWB2: 423
Communist Party and
CWB2: 417
coup attempt and *CWB2:*
422
early life of *CWB2:*
416–17
early warning systems and
CWB2: 421
Eastern Bloc and *CWB2:*
421–22
economy and *CWB2:* 418
election of *CWB2:* 422,
423
as foreign minister
CWB2: 422
on freedom *CWB2:* 416
Georgia and *CWB2:* 417,
422–23
glasnost and *CWB2:* 416
Gorbachev, Mikhail, and
CWB1: 151, 154, 166;
CWB2: 395, 418
Intermediate-range Nuclear Force treaty and
CWB2: 420
nuclear weapons and
CWB2: 418–20, 421
perestroika and *CWB2:*
416
Persian Gulf War and
CWB2: 421
religion and *CWB2:* 422
resignation of *CWB2:* 422
Shultz, George, and
CWB2: 418–20
Strategic Defense Initiative and *CWB2:* 421
Shevardnadze, Nanuli
CWB2: 423
Shriver, R. Sargent *CWA2:*
255
Shultz, George *CWA2:*
332–33, 344, 352;
CWB1: 166; *CWB2:*

418–20; *CWPS:* 283,
300, 303
Sian Incident *CWB1:* 94–96
Sidey, Hugh *CWPS:* 225–26
Signals intelligence (SIGINT)
CWA2: 224, 225;
CWPS: 233–34, 250. *See
also* Listening stations
Silent Majority *CWA2:* 276,
288–89; *CWB2:* 359
"The Sinews of Peace
speech" *CWPS:* 4,
12–13, 16–24
Sino-Soviet Treaty *CWA1:*
42, 184; *CWB2:*
316–17; *CWPS:* 69
SIS. *See* Secret Intelligence
Service (SIS)
Six Pillars of Peace CWB1:
126
Six-Day War *CWB1:* 203
Slansky, Rudolf *CWB2:*
434–35
Smith Act *CWA1:* 104, 107,
112; *CWPS:* 146, 147
Smith, Herbert *CWB2:*
367–68
Smythe, H. D. *CWB2:* 374
(ill.)
Social Democratic Labor
Party *CWA1:* 6
Socialism *CWPS:* 16, 128
Allende, Salvador, and
CWB1: 17, 18, 19–20,
21–22
Attlee, Clement R., and
CWB1: 26, 28–29
in Chile *CWB1:* 21–22;
CWB2: 263
definition of *CWB1:* 17
democracy and *CWB1:*
17, 20
economy and *CWB1:* 86
in Great Britain *CWB1:*
25, 28–29; *CWB2:*
439–40
Socialist Party *CWB1:* 18, 19
Socialist Republic of Vietnam (SRV) *CWB1:* 182
Society for Ethical Culture
CWB2: 367
Solidarity *CWA2:* 357–58;
CWB2: 394

Solomatin, Boris Aleksandrovich *CWA1:* 157
Solzhenitsyn, Aleksandr
CWA2: 293, 349;
CWB2: 234, 413
Somalia *CWA2:* 325–26;
CWB1: 50, 60
Sombolay, Albert *CWA1:*
161
Somoza, Anastasio (father)
CWA1: 180
Somoza, Anastasio (son)
CWA1: 180; *CWA2:*
330–31
Song of Russia CWB2: 384;
CWPS: 124, 135–36,
137–38
Soong Ch'ing'ling *CWB1:*
95
Soong Mei-ling. *See* Chiang
Kai-shek, Madame
Sorensen, Theodore C.
CWPS: 258
"The Sources of Soviet Conduct" *CWA1:* 35–36;
CWB2: 212; *CWPS:* 9,
11, 13
South Africa *CWA2:* 373;
CWB1: 91; *CWB2:* 310
South Korea *CWA1:* 45,
46–48, 50 (ill.), 176;
CWA2: 324; *CWB2:*
242–43, 244, 246, 247,
297–98; *CWPS:* 77, 79
South Vietnam *CWB2:* 257
Southeast Asia Treaty Organization (SEATO)
CWA1: 168, 182, 183
(ill.); *CWB1:* 130, 141
Soviet Academy of Sciences
CWB2: 410
Soviet Union *CWA2:* 350
(ill.). *See also* Commonwealth of Independent
States (CIS); Russia
Adenauer, Konrad, and
CWB1: 12, 13–14
Afghanistan and *CWA2:*
335–36, 337, 351,
355–56; *CWB1:* 50, 70,
78, 156, 164; *CWB2:*
252, 392–93, 413, 420;
CWPS: 284, 294

agriculture in *CWB1:* 44, 46; *CWB2:* 232, 238, 239, 278, 348, 429; *CWPS:* 175, 181, 189, 199

Angola and *CWA2:* 326–27; *CWB1:* 50

Asia and *CWPS:* 68

Berlin and *CWA1:* 61–62, 65–66, 111; *CWB1:* 137

Bevin, Ernest, and *CWB1:* 36–37

Big Three and *CWA1:* 2, 9–10

Brandt, Willy, and *CWB1:* 15, 48

Bretton Woods Conference and *CWA1:* 12

Brezhnev Doctrine and *CWA2:* 298, 300; *CWPS:* 274

brinkmanship and *CWPS:* 120

Bush, George, and *CWA2:* 369–70; *CWB1:* 57, 58; *CWB2:* 420, 421; *CWPS:* 294–97, 303–4, 305, 307–18

Byrnes, James F., and *CWB1:* 62, 65–68

capitalism and *CWA2:* 304, 352, 361, 367–68; *CWB2:* 280–82

Carter, Jimmy, and *CWA2:* 335–36; *CWB1:* 50, 70, 74–75, 77–78; *CWB2:* 393

Castro, Fidel, and *CWB1:* 86, 87, 88–89, 91; *CWPS:* 232, 233

Castro, Raúl, and *CWB1:* 88

Chiang Kai-shek and *CWB1:* 93

China and *CWA1:* 40–42, 52, 111, 184–85; *CWA2:* 205–6, 265–66, 300–301, 301–2, 327, 356; *CWB1:* 47, 93, 116, 118; *CWB2:* 235, 280, 316–18, 471; *CWPS:* 65, 68, 69, 70, 264, 274, 294

Churchill, Winston, and *CWB1:* 108

Clifford, Clark M., and *CWB1:* 110–11

collectivism in *CWB2:* 429

communism in *CWA1:* 27–29; *CWA2:* 299; *CWB1:* 26, 110, 127; *CWB2:* 385, 410, 418; *CWPS:* 5–14, 72, 73–76, 168–70

Communist Party in *CWA1:* 120, 121, 170, 188; *CWA2:* 241, 254–55, 260, 338, 347, 348–49, 360–62, 367–69, 372; *CWB1:* 41, 42, 43–46, 49–50, 153–54, 157, 162–63; *CWB2:* 231–32, 233, 234, 239–40, 277, 278–79, 279–80, 347, 353, 410, 417–18, 419, 429, 430, 433; *CWPS:* 174–75, 176–77, 181–82, 296, 315

composition of *CWA1:* 1, 7

Congo and *CWA2:* 208

Congress of People's Deputies in *CWA2:* 360–61; *CWB1:* 154, 157

constitution of *CWA2:* 360; *CWB1:* 154; *CWPS:* 304–5

Council of the Federation in *CWB1:* 154

coup attempt in *CWA2:* 368–69; *CWPS:* 296, 320

coup d'état in *CWB1:* 45–46, 58, 157; *CWB2:* 419, 422

Cuba and *CWA2:* 209–10, 216, 217, 219–21, 258, 273, 310; *CWB1:* 82, 86, 87, 88–91; *CWB2:* 223, 226–27; *CWPS:* 232, 233–34, 256–57, 259, 263

Cuban Missile Crisis and *CWA2:* 219–20, 226, 227, 228, 229, 260; *CWPS:* 246–49

culture in *CWA2:* 292–93, 338

Czechoslovakia and *CWA1:* 34; *CWA2:* 268; *CWB1:* 43, 47, 164, 204; *CWB2:* 216, 281, 282, 449

democracy and *CWA2:* 347, 360–61, 367–68; *CWB1:* 154; *CWB2:* 408, 415, 418; *CWPS:* 54, 56

Deng Xiaoping and *CWB1:* 118

de-Stalinization of *CWA2:* 192–93, 265–66; *CWB1:* 118; *CWB2:* 233, 236

détente and *CWA2:* 297–98, 304–5, 310, 311; *CWB1:* 48–49

disarmament and *CWPS:* 94–95, 286, 287–96, 299–300, 302–4, 305–6, 314

domino theory and *CWPS:* 221–22

Dubcek, Alexander, and *CWB1:* 47

East Berlin and *CWA1:* 69–71

East Germany and *CWA1:* 68, 69–71; *CWA2:* 358–59; *CWB1:* 58, 129–30; *CWB2:* 224–25; *CWPS:* 207, 208, 209, 210, 230

Eastern Bloc and *CWA2:* 193–96, 349; *CWB2:* 351, 446–48, 458; *CWPS:* 17–18, 30, 36, 45, 54, 56, 108

economy of *CWA1:* 17, 174–75; *CWA2:* 277, 278, 290–92, 303, 304, 337, 338, 343, 347–52, 361, 362, 367–68; *CWB1:* 3, 46, 51, 56, 146, 154–55, 157; *CWB2:* 239, 277, 279,

military and *CWA1:* 50–52; *CWA2:* 355–56; *CWB1:* 47, 51, 58; *CWB2:* 213, 239–40; *CWPS:* 99, 175, 186–87, 190–91, 193–94, 202, 211, 214–15, 221, 265

military-industrial complexes in *CWA2:* 277, 278

Molotov Plan and *CWA1:* 32–34

morality and *CWPS:* 284

most-favored-nation trade status of *CWA2:* 336, 362; *CWPS:* 309–11

nation building and *CWA1:* 180; *CWA2:* 202, 203, 254, 307–8, 325–27; *CWB1:* 50, 164

nationalization in *CWB2:* 380–81

Nazi-Soviet Non-Aggression Pact and *CWA1:* 6–8, 10

Nicaragua and *CWA2:* 331

Nixon, Richard M., and *CWB1:* 48–49, 164–65; *CWB2:* 261–62, 354, 359, 360–61; *CWPS:* 275, 280

North Atlantic Treaty Organization (NATO) and *CWA1:* 173; *CWA2:* 363–64; *CWB1:* 113; *CWB2:* 317, 441–42

North Korea and *CWB2:* 242, 243, 245–46

North Vietnam and *CWB2:* 257

nuclear energy and *CWB2:* 289–91; *CWPS:* 23

nuclear weapons and *CWA1:* 22, 43, 70, 88–91, 95–96, 115, 135–40, 174–75; *CWA2:* 200–201, 235, 236–37, 240–41, 244–45, 247, 256–58, 303–4, 305, 323, 330, 336–39, 349, 362, 364, 369–70, 372;

CWB1: 6, 47, 48–49, 50, 56, 58, 70, 77–78, 88–91, 154–55, 164–65, 166, 204; *CWB2:* 213, 226–28, 235, 238–39, 283, 285–88, 289–91, 333, 351, 360–61, 373, 375, 395–96, 409, 410–11, 418, 421, 432, 433, 434, 440–41; *CWPS:* 69, 71, 94–95, 102, 113, 114, 116–17, 120–21, 175, 190–91, 220, 265–66, 280, 284–92, 293, 295, 296, 299–300, 302–4, 308, 314

October War and *CWA2:* 309–10; *CWB1:* 50; *CWB2:* 262–63

oil and *CWB2:* 262–63

Palestine Liberation Organization and *CWB1:* 50

peace and *CWPS:* 53–54, 55–56, 99, 101–2, 103–10, 213–14, 294, 298–99, 300–302, 314

perestroika in *CWA2:* 348, 351, 358, 361; *CWB1:* 146, 153; *CWB2:* 414, 416, 418; *CWPS:* 300–301, 302, 309, 312–13

Poland and *CWA1:* 9, 10, 11, 12–13, 57; *CWA2:* 358; *CWB1:* 36–37, 51, 66, 161, 166, 171; *CWB2:* 394, 431; *CWPS:* 20

Potsdam Conference and *CWA1:* 13–17

Presidential Council in *CWB1:* 154

racism and *CWA2:* 282–83

Reagan, Ronald, and *CWA2:* 342; *CWB1:* 56, 155–56, 166, 175; *CWB2:* 216, 252, 392–93, 395–96; *CWPS:* 282–92, 293–94, 295, 312

religion in *CWB2:* 234; *CWPS:* 138, 151

reparations and *CWA1:* 15–17, 57; *CWB1:* 66

republics of *CWA2:* 361–62; *CWB2:* 417, 420–21, 422; *CWPS:* 296, 315, 317–18, 319, 320

Rice, Condoleezza, and *CWB2:* 401, 403–5

Romania and *CWB1:* 43

Roosevelt, Franklin D., and *CWA1:* 5; *CWB2:* 209

school in *CWB1:* 148–49

Sino-Soviet Treaty and *CWB2:* 316–17; *CWPS:* 69

Six-Day War and *CWB1:* 203

Somalia and *CWB1:* 50

South Korea and *CWPS:* 77

Soviet Central Committee in *CWA1:* 121

space programs and *CWB1:* 47, 142; *CWB2:* 235, 307

Strategic Arms Limitation Talks and *CWB1:* 204

Strategic Defense Initiative and *CWB2:* 393, 421; *CWPS:* 282–83, 285, 287–92

strength and *CWA1:* 70

Suez War and *CWA2:* 203; *CWB1:* 132, 142

as superpower *CWA1:* 1, 27, 37, 128; *CWB1:* 111; *CWB2:* 432; *CWPS:* 2–3, 7, 20, 102, 270

Supreme Soviet in *CWPS:* 5

Syria and *CWB1:* 50

Thatcher, Margaret, and *CWB2:* 438, 440–43

Third World and *CWA2:* 210, 254, 321–22, 349, 351; *CWB1:* 50, 164; *CWB2:* 440; *CWPS:* 283–84

espionage and *CWA1:* 140, 142–43

Foster, William Z., and *CWPS:* 160

freedom and *CWA1:* 100, 120; *CWPS:* 2

as general secretary *CWB2:* 429

Germany and *CWB2:* 432

Gorbachev, Mikhail, and *CWB1:* 150

Great Terror of *CWA1:* 120–23, 188; *CWA2:* 192–93; *CWB1:* 42–43, 45, 147–48, 160; *CWB2:* 209, 232, 236, 278, 279–80, 348, 351, 352, 370, 409–10, 412, 420, 430, 434–35; *CWPS:* 175, 176–83

Greece and *CWPS:* 34, 41

Harriman, W. Averell, and *CWB1:* 170, 171

Hitler, Adolf, and *CWB2:* 348, 431

Ho Chi Minh and *CWB1:* 183

International Monetary Fund and *CWPS:* 23

Iron Curtain and *CWA1:* 21; *CWPS:* 23

isolationism and *CWA1:* 22

Japan and *CWB1:* 66; *CWB2:* 432

Jews and *CWA1:* 121–23; *CWB2:* 435

Kennan, George F., and *CWB2:* 209–10, 211

KGB (Soviet secret police) and *CWA1:* 127, 132

Khrushchev, Nikita, and *CWA1:* 188; *CWA2:* 192–93, 265–66, 292; *CWB1:* 46, 118; *CWB2:* 230, 231–32, 233, 236, 291, 352, 419, 435–36, 471; *CWPS:* 174–75, 176–83

Kim Il Sung and *CWB2:* 243

Kosygin, Aleksey, and *CWB2:* 278–79, 279–80

Kurchatov, Igor, and *CWB2:* 285–86

Lenin, Vladimir I., and *CWB2:* 427, 428–29; *CWPS:* 178

loyalty programs and *CWA1:* 120

Maclean, Donald, and *CWA1:* 142–43

Mao Zedong and *CWA1:* 40; *CWPS:* 65, 69

Marshall Plan and *CWA1:* 34; *CWPS:* 30, 48

military and *CWA1:* 50–52; *CWB2:* 431; *CWPS:* 186–87

Molotov, Vyacheslav, and *CWB2:* 345, 346, 347–48, 351, 352

nationalism of *CWB2:* 428

Nazi-Soviet Non-Aggression Pact and *CWA1:* 6–7, 10

North Atlantic Treaty Organization and *CWB2:* 317

Novikov, Nikolai V., and *CWPS:* 4

"Novikov Telegram" and *CWPS:* 30

nuclear energy and *CWPS:* 23

nuclear weapons and *CWA1:* 9, 14, 88–89; *CWB2:* 285, 351, 432

paranoia of *CWB2:* 434, 435; *CWPS:* 179–80

Philby, Kim, and *CWA1:* 143

Poland and *CWA1:* 9, 11; *CWB1:* 66

Potsdam Conference and *CWA1:* 14–17; *CWB1:* 66; *CWB2:* 351, 431

reputation of *CWB2:* 430

Roosevelt, Franklin D., and *CWB1:* 105–6; *CWB2:* 430, 431–32

as secretary *CWB2:* 347–48

Sino-Soviet Treaty and *CWB2:* 317; *CWPS:* 69

Tehran Conference and *CWB2:* 431

Tito, Josip Broz, and *CWB2:* 434, 444, 446–48; *CWPS:* 180

Trotsky, Leon, and *CWB2:* 429

Truman, Harry S., and *CWA1:* 86; *CWB2:* 351, 452, 457; *CWPS:* 23

"Two Camps" speech of *CWA1:* 19; *CWPS:* 5

United Nations and *CWA1:* 12

United States of America and *CWPS:* 2

Warsaw Pact and *CWPS:* 186

World Bank and *CWPS:* 23

World War II and *CWB1:* 170; *CWB2:* 348, 349, 425, 430–32

Yalta agreements and *CWA1:* 2, 11, 105

Yalta Conference and *CWB1:* 65, 66; *CWB2:* 431, 432; *CWPS:* 18

Yugoslavia and *CWA1:* 51, 121

Zhou Enlai *CWB2:* 471

Star Wars. *See* Strategic Defense Initiative (SDI)

START. *See* Strategic Arms Reduction Talks (START)

Steadman, James *CWPS:* 143 (ill.)

Stephens, Mark *CWB1:* 33

Stevenson, Adlai *CWA1:* 48; *CWB1:* 140, 141–42, 173; *CWB2:* 461

Stone, Harlan Fiske *CWB2:* 456 (ill.)

Strategic Air Command (SAC)

Bush, George, and *CWA2:* 369

Cuban Missile Crisis and *CWA2:* 225

definition of *CWA1:* 80; *CWA2:* 234

early warning systems and *CWA2:* 240
formation of *CWA1:* 92
nuclear accidents and *CWA2:* 243
nuclear weapons and *CWA2:* 237–38, 239
Strategic arms *CWA2:* 234, 235
Strategic Arms Limitation Talks (SALT) *CWA2:* 307 (ill.), 331 (ill.); *CWPS:* 280, 285, 287–92
Brezhnev, Leonid, and *CWA2:* 304, 323, 330; *CWB1:* 48, 49, 50, 77–78, 166; *CWB2:* 261, 360–61
Carter, Jimmy, and *CWA2:* 323, 330, 336; *CWB1:* 49, 70, 77–78, 166; *CWB2:* 392
definition of *CWA2:* 298, 320
description of *CWA2:* 302–5
détente and *CWA2:* 297–98, 304–5
Ford, Gerald, and *CWB1:* 166
Gromyko, Andrey, and *CWB1:* 164–65, 166
Johnson, Lyndon B., and *CWB1:* 204
Kissinger, Henry, and *CWB2:* 255, 261
location of *CWA2:* 248
Nixon, Richard M., and *CWA2:* 304; *CWB1:* 48, 164–65; *CWB2:* 261, 360–61
Reagan, Ronald, and *CWA2:* 338, 353; *CWB1:* 78; *CWB2:* 390, 392
Soviet Union and *CWB1:* 204
U.S. Congress and *CWA2:* 330, 335, 336; *CWB1:* 77–78
Strategic Arms Reduction Talks (START) *CWA2:* 352, 357, 372

Strategic Defense Initiative (SDI) *CWA2:* 342–45, 352, 353 (ill.), 354; *CWPS:* 282–83, 285, 287–92, 320, 323
Baker, James, and *CWB2:* 421
Gorbachev, Mikhail, and *CWB1:* 155; *CWB2:* 395–96
Kohl, Helmut, and *CWB2:* 273
Reagan, Ronald, and *CWB1:* 155; *CWB2:* 273, 393, 395–96
Shevardnadze, Eduard, and *CWB2:* 421
Soviet Union and *CWB2:* 421
Strategic Triad *CWA2:* 234, 235, 238–40
Strauss, Lewis *CWB2:* 376; *CWPS:* 117 (ill.)
Strength *CWB1:* 1; *CWB2:* 409, 411
containment and *CWA1:* 93
freedom and *CWPS:* 278
"Iron Curtain speech" and *CWPS:* 26
Khrushchev, Nikita, and *CWA1:* 70
"Long Telegram" and *CWPS:* 18, 26
of North Atlantic Treaty Organization (NATO) *CWA1:* 185
of nuclear weapons *CWA1:* 79, 88, 95; *CWA2:* 219, 240–41
peace and *CWPS:* 189
Truman, Harry S., and *CWA1:* 22–23; *CWPS:* 23, 25–26, 30
Stripling, Robert E. *CWPS:* 137–38, 139 (ill.), 139–41, 143 (ill.)
Stroessner, Alfredo *CWA1:* 180
Submarines *CWA2:* 243 (ill.); *CWB1:* 72; *CWB2:* 309
cost of *CWA2:* 372

Cuba and *CWA2:* 310
missiles and *CWA2:* 239–40, 244
nuclear powered *CWA2:* 237
Subversives *CWA1:* 104, 107; *CWB2:* 333
Suez War *CWA2:* 203, 203 (ill.); *CWB1:* 131–32, 142; *CWB2:* 306–7
Sullivan, Kevin *CWPS:* 258, 259
Summer of love *CWA2:* 287
Sun Yat-sen *CWB1:* 93, 95; *CWB2:* 315
Supreme Soviet *CWB1:* 163; *CWPS:* 5
SVR (Russian Foreign Intelligence Service) *CWA1:* 132
Swimming *CWB2:* 318
Syngman Rhee *CWA1:* 45; CWB2: 297–98; *CWPS:* 79
Syria *CWA2:* 204, 309–10; *CWB1:* 50, 203
Szilard, Leo *CWA1:* 81

T

Tactical Air Command (TAC) *CWA2:* 225
Tactical arms *CWA2:* 234, 235
Taft, Robert A. *CWA1:* 48
Taiwan *CWB1:* 98–99, 130; *CWB2:* 469; *CWPS:* 276, 278. *See also* China; People's Republic of China (PRC); Republic of China (ROC)
China and *CWA1:* 50, 183–85; *CWA2:* 205, 266, 301
Communist Party and *CWA1:* 184–85
Eisenhower, Dwight D., and *CWA1:* 184
formation of *CWA1:* 41
Nationalists in *CWA1:* 50
Nixon, Richard M., and *CWA2:* 301

Truman, Harry S., and *CWA1:* 50

Taiwan Resolution *CWA1:* 184

Taylor, Maxwell *CWA2:* 222; *CWPS:* 238

Teachers *CWA1:* 115

Teach-ins *CWA2:* 284, 285

Tehran Conference *CWA1:* 143; *CWB1:* 105, 161; *CWB2:* 349, 431, 446; *CWPS:* 19 (ill.)

Telegraph *CWB2:* 208

Television *CWA1:* 110; *CWB1:* 143

Teller, Edward *CWA1:* 81, 94; *CWA2:* 353 (ill.); *CWB2:* 375

Terrorism *CWA2:* 376; *CWB2:* 246, 264–65, 398–99, 407; *CWPS:* 324, 325

Tet Offensive *CWA2:* 271–72; *CWB1:* 114, 183, 203–4

Texas *CWB1:* 54–55

Thant, U *CWPS:* 249

Thatcher, Denis *CWB2:* 441 (ill.)

Thatcher, Margaret *CWA1:* 144; *CWA2:* 352; *CWB2:* 272, 437 (ill.), **437–43,** 441 (ill.)

Thatcher's Law *CWB2:* 440

Thermonuclear bombs *CWA1:* 88. *See also* Nuclear weapons

Third World *CWPS:* 283–84 in Africa *CWA2:* 206 Brezhnev, Leonid, and *CWB1:* 50 Carter, Jimmy, and *CWA2:* 325 communism and *CWA1:* 176–78; *CWA2:* 193 definition of *CWA1:* 168; *CWA2:* 193, 252, 307, 321–22, 349 economy and *CWA2:* 252, 254, 307 Eisenhower, Dwight D., and *CWB1:* 141

Four Point Program and *CWA1:* 49–50 Gromyko, Andrey, and *CWB1:* 164 Khrushchev, Nikita, and *CWA2:* 210 Kim Il Sung and *CWB2:* 246 Maoism and *CWB2:* 312–13 nation building and *CWA1:* 175–82; *CWA2:* 254, 307–8, 325–27; *CWB1:* 50, 83 North Korea and *CWB2:* 246 Peace Corps and *CWA2:* 255 Reagan, Ronald, and *CWB2:* 397–99 Soviet Union and *CWA2:* 210, 254, 321–22, 349, 351; *CWB1:* 50, 164; *CWB2:* 440 United Nations and *CWA2:* 210

Thirteen Days: A Memoir of the Cuban Missile Crisis *CWPS:* 234, **236–43**

Thomas, J. Parnell *CWPS:* 139 (ill.)

Threats *CWB1:* 42, 150, 190; *CWB2:* 263 asymmetrical response and *CWA1:* 173–75 Berlin airlift and *CWA1:* 64–65 Byrnes, James F., and *CWPS:* 12 Cuban Missile Crisis and *CWA2:* 226, 227 Iran occupation and *CWPS:* 12, 14, 23 Kennan, George F., and *CWPS:* 10, 12 Kennedy, John F., and *CWPS:* 219–21 Khrushchev, Nikita, and *CWA1:* 69–71; *CWPS:* 214–15, 219–21, 234 "Long Telegram" on *CWPS:* 10

nuclear weapons and *CWA1:* 32, 64–65, 184; *CWA2:* 205, 256, 338; *CWPS:* 29, 119 press and *CWPS:* 29 as weapon *CWA1:* 2, 28, 56, 80, 100, 126, 127, 168; *CWA2:* 192, 234, 252, 276, 298, 320, 348

Thule Accident *CWA2:* 243

Thurmond, Strom *CWB2:* 460

Tiananmen Square *CWA2:* 295 (ill.), 362; *CWB1:* 121; *CWB2:* 314, 315 (ill.)

Time *CWA2:* 361; *CWB2:* 324; *CWPS:* 317

Tito, Josip Broz *CWA1:* 51, 51 (ill.), 121, 188; *CWB2:* 214 (ill.), 215–16, 434, 444 (ill.), **444–51,** 447 (ill.), 449 (ill.); *CWPS:* 34, 41, 180

Titoism *CWB2:* 448

Tocqueville, Alexis de *CWA1:* 1

Tradecraft *CWA1:* 136–37, 137 (ill.), 141

Trades Union Congress (TUC) *CWB1:* 35

Transport and General Workers' Union *CWB1:* 35

Transportation *CWA1:* 68–69, 70, 71; *CWB2:* 455

Travel *CWB2:* 225; *CWPS:* 151

Treason *CWPS:* 162–63

Treaty of Versailles *CWB1:* 126; *CWB2:* 464

Treaty on the Final Settlement with Respect to Germany *CWA2:* 364; *CWB2:* 274

Trilateral Commission *CWA2:* 321

Trinity *CWA1:* 79, 82 (ill.), 85, 87; *CWB2:* 371, 372

Trotsky, Leon *CWA1:* 4 (ill.); *CWB2:* 429

Truman, Bess *CWB2:* 456
(ill.)

Truman Committee *CWB2:*
455–56

Truman Doctrine *CWA1:* 2,
23–24, 107; *CWPS:* 30,
32–33, **34–42**
Acheson, Dean G., and
CWB1: 3–4
Clifford, Clark M., and
CWB1: 109, 111–12
communism and *CWB1:*
3–4
containment and *CWB1:*
3–4, 29–30, 38, 112,
172
Greece and *CWB1:* 112
Kennan, George F., and
CWB2: 212
"Long Telegram" and
CWB2: 212
Truman, Harry S., and
CWB1: 112, 172;
CWB2: 458–59
Turkey and *CWB1:* 112

Truman, Harry S. *CWA1:*
14 (ill.), 16 (ill.); *CWB1:*
30 (ill.), 67 (ill.); *CWB2:*
300 (ill.), 326 (ill.), 452
(ill.), **452–62,** 456 (ill.),
457 (ill.); *CWPS:* 22
(ill.), 35 (ill.), 39 (ill.),
55 (ill.), 59 (ill.), 77
(ill.), 80 (ill.)
Acheson, Dean G., and
CWB1: 3
African Americans and
CWB2: 460
Attlee, Clement R., and
CWA1: 86; *CWB1:* 31
Berlin airlift and *CWB2:*
459
Byrnes, James F., and
CWB1: 62, 65, 67–68,
127
character of *CWA1:* 25;
CWB2: 455, 461
Chiang Kai-shek and
CWB1: 96, 98
China and *CWA1:* 40, 42;
CWB1: 96, 98, 139;
CWB2: 298, 324, 467;

CWPS: 62, 65, 67–68,
101
China Lobby and *CWPS:*
62, 65
Churchill, Winston, and
CWB1: 107–8; *CWB2:*
457; *CWPS:* 12, 16
Clifford, Clark M., and
CWB1: 109, 110
Cold War and *CWA1:* 24,
25, 52; *CWB2:* 452,
458–59, 459–61, 462
containment and *CWA1:*
29–30, 168–69, 173–74;
CWB1: 3–4, 29–30, 38,
128, 172; *CWB2:*
458–59; *CWPS:* 33,
52–59, 62
death of *CWB2:* 461
Dulles, John Foster, and
CWB1: 127, 128
early life of *CWB2:*
453–54
economy and *CWB2:* 459
Eisenhower, Dwight D.,
and *CWB1:* 139;
CWPS: 100
elections of *CWB2:* 389,
455, 456, 459, 460;
CWPS: 28, 101
espionage and *CWA1:*
140, 142
Executive Order 9835
CWA1: 107
Fair Deal of *CWB2:* 459
Germany and *CWB1:* 107
Greece and *CWB1:* 29–30,
38; *CWB2:* 326; *CWPS:*
32–33, 34–41
imperialism and *CWPS:*
26
Indochina and *CWA1:* 50
Iron Curtain and *CWA1:*
20–21
"Iron Curtain speech" and
CWPS: 23, 24, 29
Israel and *CWB1:* 37;
CWB2: 326–27, 460
Japan and *CWB1:* 128
Kennan, George F., and
CWB2: 212
Kennedy, John F., and
CWB2: 220

Korea and *CWB2:* 242
Korean War and *CWA1:*
46, 47, 48; *CWB1:* 5,
98, 139–40; *CWB2:*
299–301, 461; *CWPS:*
62–63, 77, 79–80, 86,
101, 110
Lend-Lease program and
CWB1: 171
"Long Telegram" and
CWB2: 212
MacArthur, Douglas, and
CWB1: 5, 40; *CWB2:*
297, 298, 299–301, 327,
461; *CWPS:* 62–63,
80–81, 86
Mao Zedong and *CWA1:*
40, 42
Marshall, George C., and
CWB2: 324, 326–27
Marshall Plan and *CWA1:*
32; *CWB2:* 459; *CWPS:*
33, 52–59
McCarthy, Joseph R., and
CWA1: 117; *CWB1:*
140; *CWB2:* 299–300,
334, 460, 461; *CWPS:*
171
middle initial of *CWB2:*
453
military and *CWPS:*
76–77
Molotov, Vyacheslav, and
CWB2: 350–51
National Security Act and
CWA1: 34
Nitze, Paul H., and *CWPS:*
69, 71
North Atlantic Treaty Or-
ganization (NATO) and
CWA1: 37–38; *CWB2:*
459; *CWPS:* 100
NSC-68 and *CWA1:* 45,
46, 173; *CWPS:* 76–77
nuclear weapons and
CWA1: 13–14, 43, 86,
88, 91, 92–95, 115–16;
CWB1: 3, 31, 108;
CWB2: 212, 288, 333,
351, 375, 458; *CWPS:*
69
Office of Strategic Services
(OSS) and *CWA1:* 130

Oppenheimer, J. Robert, and *CWB2:* 373

peace and *CWPS:* 38, 53–54, 54–56, 57

Pendergast, Thomas, and *CWB2:* 454

political beginnings of *CWB2:* 454–55

popularity of *CWB2:* 459, 460, 461, 462

Potsdam Conference and *CWA1:* 13–17; *CWB1:* 65, 66; *CWB2:* 351, 431, 457

presidency of *CWB2:* 452, 456–62

Reagan, Ronald, and *CWB2:* 389

Red Scare and *CWA1:* 106, 107, 108, 117

Republic of China and *CWB1:* 39, 98, 118; *CWPS:* 69, 70

retirement of *CWB2:* 461

Rio Pact and *CWB2:* 459

Roosevelt, Franklin D., and *CWB1:* 65; *CWB2:* 455, 456

Rusk, Dean, and *CWB1:* 202

as senator *CWB2:* 455–56

Smith Act and *CWA1:* 107

Soviet Union and *CWB1:* 171–72; *CWB2:* 288, 333; *CWPS:* 23, 25–26, 28, 30

"Special Message to the Congress on Greece and Turkey: The Truman Doctrine, March 12, 1947" *CWPS:* 34–42

"Special Message to the Congress on the Threat to the Freedom of Europe, March 17, 1948" *CWPS:* 52–60

Stalin, Joseph, and *CWA1:* 86; *CWB2:* 351, 452, 457; *CWPS:* 23

strength and *CWA1:* 22–23; *CWPS:* 23, 25–26, 30

Taiwan and *CWA1:* 50

Tito, Josip Broz, and *CWB2:* 448

transportation and *CWB2:* 455

Truman Committee and *CWB2:* 455–56

Truman Doctrine and *CWA1:* 2, 23–24, 107; *CWB1:* 29–30, 38, 112, 172; *CWB2:* 212, 458–59; *CWPS:* 33, **34–42**

Turkey and *CWB1:* 29–30, 38; *CWB2:* 326; *CWPS:* 32–33; *CWPS:* 34–41

United Nations and *CWB2:* 457; *CWPS:* 38, 96

U.S. Congress and *CWPS:* 32–33, 36–41

Vietnam and *CWA1:* 42

Wallace, Henry A. *CWB2:* 461; *CWPS:* 30

World War I and *CWB2:* 454

World War II and *CWA1:* 10–11, 18, 86; *CWB1:* 106–7; *CWB2:* 455–56, 457–58

Yalta agreements and *CWA1:* 11

Yalta Conference and *CWB1:* 65

Yugoslavia and *CWA1:* 51

Zhou Enlai and *CWB2:* 468–69

TRW *CWA1:* 154–55

TUC. *See* Trades Union Congress (TUC)

Tupolev, A. N. *CWB2:* 290 (ill.)

Turkey *CWB1:* 3–4, 29–30, 38, 112; *CWB2:* 326; *CWPS:* 32–33, 34–41, 234, 255

Cuban Missile Crisis and *CWA2:* 228, 229–30, 260

Great Britain and *CWA1:* 23

Soviet Union and *CWA1:* 18–19, 23

Truman Doctrine and *CWA1:* 2

26th of July Movement *CWB1:* 85

"Two Camps" speech *CWA1:* 19; *CWPS:* 5

Tydings, Millard *CWA1:* 117

U

U-2 aircraft *CWA1:* 147 (ill.)

Cuban Missile Crisis and *CWA2:* 225, 228

definition of *CWA1:* 127

espionage and *CWA1:* 127, 147–50; *CWA2:* 211, 240, 310

missiles and *CWA2:* 198

Powers, Francis Gary, and *CWA1:* 149–50; *CWA2:* 211, 240

U.S. Air Force and *CWA1:* 147

UAR. *See* United Arab Republic (UAR)

Ukraine *CWA1:* 7; *CWA2:* 369, 370, 373; *CWB1:* 58; *CWPS:* 317

Ulbricht, Walter *CWA1:* 57, 68, 71, 72 (ill.), 73; *CWB2:* 225

Berlin Wall and *CWPS:* 226–27

border closing by *CWPS:* 206

Khrushchev, Nikita, and *CWPS:* 207, 208, 209, 210, 215, 217, 224, 226–27

Soviet Union and *CWPS:* 207, 208, 209, 210

UN. *See* United Nations (UN)

UNESCO. *See* United Nations Educational, Scientific, and Cultural Organization (UNESCO)

Union of Soviet Socialist Republics (USSR). *See* Soviet Union

United Arab Republic (UAR) *CWA2:* 204

United Front *CWB1:* 96

United Fruit Company *CWA1:* 179, 180; *CWB1:* 86

United Nations (UN) *CWPS:* 299 (ill.)

Atomic Energy Commission *CWA1:* 18, 22

Attlee, Clement R., and *CWB1:* 28

Bevin, Ernest, and *CWA1:* 18–19

Bush, George, and *CWB1:* 55, 60

charter of *CWA1:* 12, 13

China and *CWA2:* 266, 327; *CWB1:* 98–99, 119; *CWB2:* 313, 360, 469

communism and *CWPS:* 88, 90, 91, 94, 95

composition of *CWA2:* 210

Congo and *CWA2:* 207–8

Cuba and *CWB1:* 91

Cuban Missile Crisis and *CWA2:* 226, 227; *CWPS:* 241, 248, 249

definition of *CWA1:* 2

democracy and *CWPS:* 21

Deng Xiaoping and *CWB1:* 119

Dulles, John Foster, and *CWB1:* 127

Eisenhower, Dwight D., and *CWPS:* 113–19

formation of *CWA1:* 10, 12; *CWB1:* 28, 105, 127, 161; *CWB2:* 457; *CWPS:* 90

function of *CWA1:* 12–13, 113; *CWA2:* 191

General Assembly *CWPS:* 298–306

Gorbachev, Mikhail, and *CWA2:* 355, 365; *CWB1:* 156; *CWPS:* 290, 294, 298–306

Grenada and *CWB2:* 395

Gromyko, Andrey, and *CWB1:* 161, 166

human rights and *CWA2:* 315

inspections and *CWPS:* 102, 108, 109

Iraq and *CWA2:* 365

Khrushchev, Nikita, and *CWA2:* 191, 210; *CWB2:* 233–34, 238

Kirkpatrick, Jeane, and *CWB2:* 249, 251–52, 253

Korea and *CWB2:* 243

Korean War and *CWA1:* 46–48; *CWB1:* 5; *CWB2:* 243, 299; *CWPS:* 79–80, 90–91, 94, 97

members of *CWA1:* 13

North Korea and *CWB2:* 247

nuclear energy and *CWB1:* 3; *CWB2:* 373; *CWPS:* 113–19

nuclear weapons and *CWPS:* 94–95, 102, 108, 118

October War and *CWB2:* 263

Panama invasion and *CWB1:* 60

peace and *CWPS:* 21, 22, 38, 56, 88, 90–98, 103, 108, 300–302

Persian Gulf War and *CWPS:* 317

proposal for *CWB1:* 161

Reagan, Ronald, and *CWA2:* 341, 345; *CWB2:* 395

Republic of China and *CWB1:* 98–99; *CWB2:* 469

Roosevelt, Eleanor, and *CWPS:* 88, 90–98

Roosevelt, Franklin D., and *CWA1:* 12

Security Council *CWA1:* 12, 20, 46; *CWPS:* 90–91, 248

Six-Day War and *CWB1:* 203

South Korea and *CWB2:* 247

Soviet Union and *CWB1:* 5, 66; *CWPS:* 21, 56, 94–95

Stalin, Joseph, and *CWA1:* 12

Suez War and *CWA2:* 203; *CWB1:* 132, 142

Third World and *CWA2:* 210

Truman, Harry S., and *CWB2:* 457; *CWPS:* 38, 96

UNESCO *CWA2:* 341

Universal Declaration of Human Rights *CWPS:* 90

voting in *CWA1:* 11, 12; *CWB1:* 66, 161

World War III and *CWPS:* 94, 95

Yalta Conference and *CWA1:* 12

United Nations Educational, Scientific, and Cultural Organization (UNESCO) *CWA2:* 341

United Nations Security Council *CWA1:* 12, 20, 46

Cuba and *CWB1:* 91

formation of *CWB1:* 161

United States of America. *See also* specific presidents, officials, and offices

agriculture in *CWPS:* 199

Bush, George, on *CWB1:* 53

capitalism in *CWB1:* 86, 127

Cominform in *CWPS:* 161

Communist Party in *CWB1:* 192; *CWPS:* 153–57, 159–61

democracy in *CWB1:* 25–26, 127; *CWB2:* 271

dictatorship and *CWA2:* 268, 275–77, 279, 280–81; *CWB1:* 76, 84–85; *CWB2:* 250–51, 263

economy of *CWA1:* 17; *CWA2:* 304, 338–39,

362, 372–73; *CWB1:* 3, 4, 26, 60, 64, 71, 76–77, 84–85, 86–87, 204; *CWB2:* 294–95, 323, 369–70, 389, 391, 392, 455

elections in *CWB1:* 25–26

Great Britain and *CWPS:* 21–22, 25–26, 28–29

greatness of *CWA1:* 1

Ho Chi Minh and *CWB1:* 181–82

imperialism and *CWA1:* 31–32, 33; *CWA2:* 208, 209, 217–18, 259, 269–70, 308, 322; *CWB1:* 82–83, 87, 88, 141; *CWB2:* 223, 263, 395–97; *CWPS:* 25–31

Indochina and *CWB1:* 181

isolationism and *CWA1:* 5, 6, 12, 19–20, 37, 48; *CWB1:* 170; *CWB2:* 211; *CWPS:* 2, 41, 74, 91, 93, 94, 323

population of *CWA1:* 17

Stalin, Joseph, and *CWPS:* 2

strength and *CWA1:* 22–23

as superpower *CWA1:* 1, 17, 27, 28, 128; *CWB1:* 111; *CWB2:* 324, 432; *CWPS:* 2–3, 7, 19, 102, 170, 270, 320, 321–22, 323, 325

Vietnam and *CWB1:* 181–82

World War I and *CWA1:* 5

World War II and *CWA1:* 3, 8–18, 29–30; *CWA2:* 364; *CWPS:* 7, 13–14

United States of America Medal of Merit *CWB2:* 373

Universal Declaration of Human Rights *CWPS:* 90

Uranium Committee *CWA1:* 82

U.S. Air Force *CWA2:* 237 (ill.). *See also* Military

Berlin airlift and *CWA1:* 62–66

Cuban Missile Crisis and *CWA2:* 225

nuclear accidents and *CWA2:* 242–43

nuclear weapons and *CWA1:* 174; *CWA2:* 235, 237–38

U-2 aircraft and *CWA1:* 147

U.S. Army *CWA1:* 118, 145–46, 153, 161, 172; *CWB1:* 140; *CWB2:* 244 (ill.), 323, 327, 334–35; *CWPS:* 172. *See also* Military

U.S. Army Signals Intelligence Service *CWA1:* 127, 131, 132–35

U.S. Congress *CWPS:* 35 (ill.), 85 (ill.). *See also* House Un-American Activities Committee (HUAC)

Alliance for Progress and *CWA2:* 263

Atomic Energy Commission and *CWA1:* 80, 92

Civil Defense and *CWPS:* 212–13

communism and *CWPS:* 162, 170–71

Dominican Republic and *CWA2:* 265

Eisenhower Doctrine and *CWA2:* 203–4

Eisenhower, Dwight D., and *CWPS:* 81

Four Point Program and *CWA1:* 49–50

Greece and *CWB2:* 326; *CWPS:* 32–33, 36–41

Gulf of Tonkin Resolution and *CWA2:* 270

Hatch Act and *CWA1:* 104

Intermediate-range Nuclear Force (INF) treaty and *CWA2:* 354–55

Iran-Contra scandal and *CWA2:* 332, 333

Johnson, Lyndon B., in *CWB1:* 196

Kennedy, John F., in *CWB2:* 219–21

Kirkpatrick, Jeane, and *CWB2:* 249

Kissinger, Henry, and *CWB2:* 264

MacArthur, Douglas, and *CWB2:* 300–301; *CWPS:* 63, 81–86

Marshall, George C., and *CWB2:* 326

Marshall Plan and *CWA1:* 32; *CWPS:* 33, 52–59

military and *CWPS:* 76–77

National Defense Education Act and *CWA2:* 197

National Security Act and *CWA1:* 34

Nicaragua and *CWA2:* 332; *CWB2:* 398

Nixon, Richard M., in *CWB2:* 355–56

NSC-68 and *CWA1:* 45; *CWB1:* 6; *CWPS:* 76–77

nuclear war and *CWPS:* 212–13

nuclear weapons and *CWA2:* 342; *CWB1:* 108

Peace Corps and *CWA2:* 255

perestroika and *CWPS:* 309

Red Scare and *CWA1:* 102–3, 104, 106

Smith Act and *CWA1:* 104

Strategic Arms Limitation Talks (SALT) and *CWA2:* 330, 335, 336; *CWB1:* 77–78

Strategic Defense Initiative and *CWPS:* 283, 291, 323

Taiwan and *CWA1:* 184; *CWA2:* 266

Truman Doctrine and *CWPS:* 32–33, 36–41

Truman, Harry S., and *CWPS:* 32–33, 36–41

Turkey and *CWB2:* 326;
CWPS: 32–33, 36–41
veterans and *CWB2:* 295
Vietnam War and *CWA2:*
312; *CWB1:* 199, 201
U.S. Department of Defense
CWA1: 35; *CWA2:* 198,
285; *CWB1:* 109;
CWPS: 71–72
U.S. Department of Educa-
tion *CWB1:* 76
U.S. Department of Energy
CWB1: 76
U.S. Navy *CWA1:* 155–57;
CWA2: 210, 239–40. *See
also* Military
U.S. Senate *CWB1:* 193;
CWB2: 220
U.S. State Department
CWA1: 113, 117, 118;
CWB1: 6; *CWB2:* 324,
331–32, 334
  China and *CWPS:* 65,
  67–68
  Iran occupation and
  CWPS: 12, 23
  "Long Telegram" and
  CWPS: 5
  McCarthy, Joseph R., and
  CWPS: 69, 73, 123,
  166–71
  NSC-68 and *CWPS:* 71–72
U.S. Supreme Court *CWA2:*
278
USA. *See* United States of
America (USA)
USS *Missouri CWA1:* 17, 21
(ill.); *CWPS:* 12
USS *Pueblo CWB1:* 203;
CWB2: 246
U.S.S.R. *See* Soviet Union

V

Vance, Cyrus *CWA2:* 321,
322 (ill.), 323, 325, 335;
CWB1: 74
Vardaman, James *CWB1:*
110
VENONA *CWA1:* 133 (ill.)
  atomic spies and *CWA1:*
  138

Cambridge Spies and
CWA1: 140
definition of *CWA1:* 127
overview of *CWA1:*
132–35
Philby, Kim, and *CWA1:*
143
Versailles Peace Conference
CWB1: 126, 178
Versailles Treaty *CWPS:* 20
Veterans *CWB2:* 295
Vietcong *CWA2:* 252, 269,
270, 276, 283; *CWB1:*
183, 203; *CWB2:* 258
Vietminh *CWB1:* 179, 180
Vietnam *CWA2:* 285 (ill.);
CWPS: 267. *See also*
North Vietnam; South
Vietnam
  Cambodia and *CWA2:*
  327, 328
  China and *CWA1:* 42;
  CWA2: 328; *CWB2:*
  469
  colonialism and *CWB1:*
  177–78
  communism in *CWA1:* 42
  Communist Party in
  CWB1: 176
  Declaration of Indepen-
  dence in *CWB1:*
  181–82
  division of *CWA1:*
  181–82; *CWA2:* 283;
  CWB1: 130, 141, 180,
  198; *CWB2:* 257
  domino theory and
  CWB1: 181, 198
  Dulles, John Foster, and
  CWB1: 130
  Eisenhower, Dwight D.,
  and *CWA1:* 181–82;
  CWA2: 283; *CWB1:*
  141
  elections in *CWA1:* 182
  France and *CWA1:* 42,
  181–82; *CWA2:* 283;
  CWB1: 141, 177–78,
  179, 180, 198; *CWB2:*
  257, 469
  freedom in *CWB1:*
  181–82

Great Britain and *CWB1:*
141
Ho Chi Minh and *CWA1:*
42
Japan and *CWB1:* 179
names in *CWB1:* 180
reunification of *CWB1:*
182
Soviet Union and *CWA1:*
42; *CWA2:* 328
Truman, Harry S., and
CWA1: 42
United States of America
and *CWB1:* 181–82
Zhou Enlai and *CWB2:*
469
Vietnam War *CWA2:* 271
(ill.), 284 (ill.), 285 (ill.),
286 (ill.), 289 (ill.);
CWB1: 200 (ill.)
  Acheson, Dean G., and
  CWB1: 7–8
  beginning of *CWPS:* 267
  Brezhnev, Leonid, and
  CWB1: 50
  Carter, Jimmy, and
  CWB1: 76
  causes of *CWA2:* 268–69
  chemical warfare and
  CWA2: 283–84, 290
  China and *CWA2:*
  270–71, 290, 301;
  CWPS: 267, 272,
  274–76
  Christmas bombing in
  CWA2: 313; *CWB2:*
  259, 359
  Clifford, Clark M., and
  CWB1: 109, 114–15
  communism and *CWA2:*
  283, 284, 290
  conduct of *CWA2:* 269–73
  counterculture and
  CWA2: 286–88
  death in *CWA2:* 271, 273,
  283–84, 290, 313, 372;
  CWB1: 201; *CWB2:*
  258, 359; *CWPS:*
  267–68, 324
  Democratic Party and
  CWB2: 358
  détente and *CWA2:* 312

W

CWA1: 185; CWA2: 364

Washington Dulles International Airport CWB1: 131

Watergate scandal CWA2: 298, 299, 310–11; CWB1: 55, 74; CWB2: 262, 264, 363–64; CWPS: 264–65, 282

Wauck, Bonnie CWA1: 162, 163

We the Living CWB2: 383

Weapons CWB1: 42, 150, 190. See also Missiles; Nuclear weapons
chemical CWA2: 283–84, 290; CWPS: 311
cost of CWPS: 104–5, 324
hidden CWA1: 136
inspections of CWPS: 95, 102–3, 108, 188–89, 201
peace and CWPS: 104–5, 107–8, 109
strategic arms CWA2: 234, 235
tactical arms CWA2: 234, 235
words as CWA1: 2, 28, 56, 80, 100, 126, 127, 168; CWA2: 192, 234, 252, 276, 298, 320, 348

Weinberger, Caspar CWA2: 332–33; CWB1: 60

Welch, Joseph N. CWA1: 118; CWB2: 329, 335, 335 (ill.); CWPS: 111, 172

West Berlin CWA1: 73 (ill.), 75 (ill.), 76 (ill.); CWB1: 132; CWB2: 224–25, 235–37; CWPS: 205, 210, 211–14, 222 (ill.), 224–31, 226 (ill.), 249. See also Berlin
blockades of CWA1: 37, 56, 62–66, 64 (ill.), 67 (ill.), 111
détente and CWA2: 306
Eisenhower, Dwight D., and CWA1: 70

Kennedy, John F., and CWA1: 70–71
military and CWA1: 69–71
Soviet Union and CWA1: 69–71

West Germany CWA1: 33 (ill.), 60 (ill.); CWPS: 204–5, 205–7. See also Germany
Acheson, Dean G., and CWB1: 4–5
Adenauer, Konrad, and CWB1: 9, 11–16
Brandt, Willy, and CWB1: 15
Brezhnev, Leonid, and CWB1: 47–48
capitalism and CWB2: 268
Christian Democratic Union in CWB2: 270, 271
constitution of CWB1: 11–12
democracy and CWB2: 268
Dulles, John Foster, and CWB1: 131
East Germany and CWB1: 15; CWB2: 271–72
economy of CWA1: 62–66, 67–68, 68–69; CWB1: 9, 12, 14; CWB2: 272
elections in CWA1: 67, 173; CWB1: 12, 15; CWB2: 271
espionage and CWA1: 60
formation of CWA1: 30–31, 38, 55, 60–61, 66–68, 173; CWB1: 4–5, 12, 138; CWB2: 224, 235, 268, 432
France and CWB1: 12, 13, 14
government of CWA1: 66–67
Great Britain and CWB2: 308
Gromyko, Andrey, and CWB1: 165

independence of CWB1: 13
Marshall Plan and CWA1: 67
military of CWA1: 185
North Atlantic Treaty Organization (NATO) and CWA1: 68, 173; CWB1: 12–14; CWB2: 271–72, 273
nuclear weapons and CWB2: 272–73
Ostopolitik and CWA2: 305–6
Poland and CWB1: 15
Soviet Union and CWA1: 60–62, 65–66; CWA2: 206; CWB1: 13–14, 15, 47–48, 165; CWB2: 271–72

Western European Union (WEU) CWA1: 37

Western Union CWB2: 208

Westmoreland, William C. CWA2: 271; CWB2: 342

WEU. See Western European Union (WEU)

Whalen, William Henry CWA1: 153

White Citizen's Council CWB1: 73

The White House Years CWB1: 144

White Paper CWPS: 65, 67–68, 81

Whitworth, Jerry A. CWA1: 156

"Whiz Kids" CWB2: 339

Why England Slept CWB2: 219

Wigner, Eugene CWA1: 81

Wiley, Alexander CWB2: 330–31

Will, George F. CWB2: 345

Wilson, Woodrow CWA1: 4–5; CWB1: 125

Women's rights CWB1: 63

Woodstock Festival CWA2: 287–88

World Bank CWA1: 13, 22; CWB1: 2–3; CWB2: 342; CWPS: 23

X

Y

Z